EARTH TRANSFORMED WITH MUSIC!

Inclusive Songs for Worship

Jann Aldredge-Clanton
with composer Larry E. Schultz

Published in the United States of America by Eakin Press
An Imprint of Wild Horse Media Group
P.O. Box 331779
Fort Worth, Texas 76163
1-888-982-8270
www.EakinPress.com

1 2 3 4 5 6 7 8 9
ISBN-10: 1-68179-009-2
ISBN-13: 978-1-68179-009-1
Library of Congress Control Number: 2015947893

CONTENTS

INTRODUCTION 7

GENDER EQUALITY

1. Come, Sing of New Creation
2. Renewing, Reforming the Church in Our Day
3. Mary Magdalene Inspires Us
4. Miriam Shows Us Pathways to Freedom
5. We Gather in a Circle Here

RACIAL EQUALITY

6. We Work for Racial Justice Now
7. We Long for Change
8. Follow Her Peaceful Ways
9. Our Lady Guadalupe
10. Longing to Be Free at Last

MARRIAGE EQUALITY

11. Praise the Source of All Creation
12. Rejoicing, Reclaiming Our Life-Giving Call
13. Celebrate This Congregation

14. All Day and Night Shekhinah Guides Us
15. Where She Dwells, There Is Love

ECONOMIC JUSTICE

16. Where Are Liberty and Justice?
17. We Hear the Cries of Millions
18. Rise Up and Shout
19. Join Together, Work for Justice
20. All Who Labor Through Day and Night
21. A Stranger, Starving on the Street
22. Who Will Help All Those in Need?

CARE OF CREATION

23. Praise the Source of Every Blessing
24. O Earth, We Hear Your Cries of Pain
25. Ruah, the Spirit, Dwells
26. Sophia Wisdom Shows the Way
27. Come, Join with the Children

PEACEMAKING

28. Holy Wisdom Still Is Calling
29. Sister Wisdom, Come to Guide Us
30. Hope Springs Anew
31. Shekhinah Dwells Within Our Hearts
32. Come, Mother Eagle, Show the Way

EXPANDING SPIRITUAL EXPERIENCE

33. Praise Sophia, Holy Wisdom
34. She Lives and Moves Throughout the Earth
35. Come Rejoicing, Celebrating Life Together
36. The Sacred Realm Is Like the Yeast
37. Holy, Wondrous Mystery, Birthing All Creation
38. Our Great Creator Lives in All

INTERFAITH COLLABORATION

39. In Unity We Gather
40. We Praise the Source of Life
41. Gathered Here to Share Our Music
42. From Wisdom Emerging
43. Our Mother Rock Who Gave Us Birth

COMFORT AND HEALING

44. Sophia Moves Within Our Souls
45. Gently Shaddai Comes Healing Wounded Hearts
46. Sister Friend, Brother Friend
47. Love Divine Is Like a Searching Woman
48. Wisdom Sophia Brings Us Peace

THANKSGIVING AND CELEBRATION

49. Celebrate Our Maker's Glory
50. We Come in Celebration
51. With Hearts Overflowing Our Voices We Raise
52. She Lives!
53. Come, Celebrate All Saints

SHORT SONGS FOR WORSHIP SERVICES

54. Come and Worship Our Loving Creator
55. We Come Rejoicing Here Today
56. For the Wisdom in the Word
57. Rushing Wind, Transforming Fire
58. Sister-Brother Spirit, Within Us and Above
59. Mystery Divine
60. As We Come to the Table of Love
61. We Come to This Table
62. Spirit of New Life
63. Come, Sophia Wisdom, Come
64. Go Now with Wisdom
65. Go Out with Love

Notes....97

Topical Index of Hymns....107

Index of Scripture References....146

Index of Composers, Authors, and Sources....149

Alphabetical Index of Tunes....151

Metrical Index of Tunes....153

Index of Titles....155

INTRODUCTION

The title of this new collection, *Earth Transformed with Music! Inclusive Songs for Worship,* expresses our deep belief in the power of music to transform people and all creation. Music has great power to transform our world. Music stirs our spirits and embeds words in our memories. Songs with inclusive lyrics contribute to an expansive theology and an ethic of equality and justice in human relationships.

The words we sing in worship matter. Words shape our values and drive our actions. Words we use in worship carry great power because of the sacred value given to them. Words we sing in worship have the greatest power to shape our beliefs and actions because the music ingrains the words in our hearts. We can contribute to transforming the world through music, through inclusive songs in our worship services.

In 1984, Virginia Ramey Mollenkott wrote in her book *The Divine Feminine: The Biblical Imagery of God as Female*: "It seems natural to assume that Christian people, eager to transmit the Good News that the Creator loves each human being equally and unconditionally, would be right in the vanguard of those who utilize inclusive language. Yet a visit to almost any church on Sunday morning indicates that alas, it is not happening that way." More than thirty years later, it still is not happening. The language of hymns and litanies in the majority of churches reveals worship of a male God. Biblical female divine names and imagery are still missing, and all people and all creation suffer from this exclusion. Today, as much as ever, we need inclusive worship.

Although some people use the term "inclusive" to mean "gender-neutral," we use it to mean language inclusive of all genders. We also use "expansive" and "gender-balanced" to convey this meaning. To be truly inclusive, we need what Presbyterian pastor Rebecca Kiser calls "gender-*full*" rather than "genderless" language for the Divine. Although some people consider "God," "Christ," and "Lord" to be gender-neutral, these words are usually heard as male because of centuries of association with male pronouns and imagery. Thus the gender-neutral names for Deity in this collection draw from the wealth of biblical divine names without male associations, such as "Spirit," "Maker," "Source," "Love," "Friend," and "Guide." Also, these songs give "affirmative action" to biblical female divine names and images because of their centuries-long exclusion from worship services, an exclusion that continues in most churches. These lyrics resurrect biblical female divine names, such as "Wisdom," *Sophia, Hokmah, Ruah, Shaddai, Shekhinah,* "Mother Rock," "Baker Woman," "Searching Woman," "Midwife," "Mother Hen," and "Mother Eagle." These female names of the Divine help to transform patriarchal structures that continue to support worldwide oppression of women and girls. When we include female names for Deity, then women and girls are seen in Her image and thus respected and valued, instead of oppressed and abused. Gender-balanced names and images of the Divine affirm the sacred value of all people and all creation.

Major Themes of Songs

Social justice themes are prominent in this collection, as in our other hymn collections. "What does God require of you but to do justice, and to love kindness, and to walk humbly with God" (Micah 6:8), and "Let justice roll down like waters, and righteousness like an everflowing stream" (Amos 5:24) form a biblical foundation for this emphasis on justice. Gender equality, racial equality, marriage equality, economic justice, and care of creation flow from these biblical passages. Some of the songs in this collection focus on these justice themes separately and others bring them together, recognizing the intersectionality of sexism, racism, and heterosexism, and their connection to environmental and economic justice.

The inclusive language of the songs in this collection supports gender equality. These songs use gender inclusive language for humanity and for divinity. "Renewing, Reforming the Church in Our Day," for example, pictures sisters and brothers joining "hand in hand to bring new creation throughout every land." Songs that include biblical female names and images of divinity affirm the equal value of females in the divine image. In "Come, Sing of New Creation" the biblical female divine image of "Holy Wisdom" gives us Her power to open doors for gender equality, illustrated by this concluding stanza:

Come, celebrate all pioneers who open minds and doors,
as Holy Wisdom gives us Her power evermore.
Our sons and daughters preaching stir all to dream and dare,
to co-create and nurture a world of loving care.

Several songs feature biblical women, like Mary Magdalene and Miriam. For example, "Mary Magdalene Inspires Us" celebrates the biblical accounts of Mary Magdalene as the first witness of the resurrection, the "apostle to the apostles." Positive portrayals of females in the biblical stories and biblical female images of Deity contribute to gender equality.

The songs in *Earth Transformed with Music!* also contribute to racial equality by changing the traditional symbolism of darkness as evil and light as good to symbolism of both darkness and light as good. For example, in "Wisdom Sophia Brings Us Peace" we sing of "Holy Darkness" showing the "Way." "Holy, Wondrous Mystery, Birthing All Creation" includes this stanza:

Holy, wondrous Mystery, darkness magnifies you;
in the darkened depths of soil You root and sprout and thrive;
holy, spacious Darkness, moon and sun shine through you;
stars on Your canvas bring the skies to life.

A song featuring Our Lady of Guadalupe affirms the darkness and light in Her image as reconnecting all people. "We Work for Racial Justice Now" sounds a clear call for sisters and brothers to join together to claim the "promised land" of racial equality. These lines specifically celebrate all races in the divine image:

O Sister-Brother Spirit, help us know Your breadth and height;
each culture, every color shows Your image dark and bright.

Other songs in this collection also affirm all races, along with all genders, as reflecting Divinity. In "Follow Her Peaceful Ways" Holy Wisdom blesses "all cultures, all genders and races, welcoming all in Her loving embrace."

All gender identities and sexual orientations have equal value in the divine image. The songs in this collection affirm sexual and gender diversity as sacred gifts, and marriage equality as a basic human right. "Praise the Source of All Creation," for example, concludes with this stanza:

Equal marriage, healing, freeing, nurtures body, mind, and soul,
reaffirming every being, all created good and whole.
Come, rejoice and sing together, celebrating life and love;
praise the great Creative Spirit, living in us and above.

Other songs also bless and affirm all genders, including all people who have been "excluded, judged, and scorned" by "dogma and fear" and "custom's norms." The inclusion of female divine names and imagery in this song collection also supports the inclusion of LBGTQ persons as equal participants in church and society with the right to marriage and all other human rights. Male-dominated worship language and imagery contribute to heterosexism as well as to sexism by exalting the traditional "masculine" and devaluing any traits that have been traditionally labeled "feminine." This exclusively male symbolism contributes to the demeaning, exclusion, and abuse of LGBTQ persons. But when Deity is imaged as female, as well as male and much more, then all are seen in the divine image and thus given greater value and respect.

The theme of economic justice flows through the songs in this collection, connected to equity for people of all genders, races, and sexual orientations. Some of the songs, written for workers' rights events, focus specifically on economic justice. "We Hear the Cries of Millions," for example, laments that "the rich are growing richer" while "the poor cry out in pain," and calls us to work for change:

Join hands for jobs with justice, with workers' rights ensured,
with safe and fair conditions, health care for all secured.
Come, Sister-Brother Spirit, and fill us with Your power;
inspire our words and actions in this most urgent hour.

Other songs call on Holy Wisdom for Her help in our work for economic fairness. The names and images for Deity throughout this collection of songs contribute to economic justice. Some traditional divine names and images, such as "Master," "Lord," and "King," support a hierarchical class system with rich, white, straight men dominating from the top. Multicultural female divine names and images, such as "Holy Wisdom" and "Our Lady of Guadalupe," and other non-hierarchical divine images, such as "Friend," in this song collection contribute to overcoming sexism, heterosexism, racism, and classism so that there will be economic justice for all.

Care of creation is another major theme of the songs in *Earth Transformed with Music! Inclusive Songs for Worship.* Some of the songs, written for a Faith and Feminism/Womanist/Mujerista Conference on eco-justice, focus specifically on caring for the environment. For example, in "O Earth, We Hear Your Cries of Pain" we sing of joining together to heal the earth, beginning with this stanza:

O Earth, we hear your cries of pain, your cries of desolation;
we join to heal your many wounds, to bring your restoration.
Polluted air and poisoned seas endanger all the living;
if greedy hands use up your wealth, you cannot keep on giving.

Several other songs challenge us to save creation that has been "fractured, poisoned, scarred," to work together to conserve, protect, and "save Earth's treasures." The female divine names and images in this collection of songs support caring for creation. The whole creation suffers from male-dominated theology that has at its foundation an exclusively masculine naming and imaging of Deity. References to the earth are traditionally feminine, but the feminine is not given sacred value in our worship. Like females, the earth continues to be devalued, exploited, assaulted, and abused. Biblical female names and images of the Divine in these songs, such as *Ruah* ("Spirit") and *Sophia* ("Wisdom"), connect the revaluing of females to the revaluing of the earth, contributing to overcoming sexism and exploitation of the earth.

Another main theme in this collection is peace, flowing from justice for all people and all creation. "Happy are those who find Wisdom. Her ways are ways of pleasantness, and all Her paths are peace" (Proverbs 3:13,17). Divine Wisdom and Her peaceful pathways are prominent in the songs in this collection. These songs encourage nonviolence in homes, cities, nations, and throughout the world. "Holy Wisdom Still Is Calling," for example, urges us to "work to stop the wars of nations and domestic violence end." Females and LGBTQ people suffer from gender-based violence that is still prevalent around the world. Peace is closely linked to justice for all people. Another song in this collection that emphasizes the connection between peace and justice is "Sister Wisdom, Come to Guide Us," beginning with this stanza:

Sister Wisdom, come to guide us on your healing paths of peace;
give us courage for each challenge, that your justice may increase.
Joined with you we dream and dare, all your blessings freely share.

Internal peace contributes to our peacemaking in the world. The songs in this collection nurture inner peace as well as external peace. For example, "Skekhinah Dwells Within Our Hearts" affirms the hope and peace that She brings in the midst of the "hard and long" challenges of our work for peace and justice.

Earth Transformed with Music! also contributes to expanding spiritual experience through including a wide variety of biblical names and images of the Divine. Our spirituality expands and deepens when we discover Deity as including female and male and more. Inclusive divine images empower all people to experience greater freedom to fulfill our potential in the divine image. In "Come Rejoicing, Celebrating Life Together" we sing of reforming and transforming the church with this "wider view," inspiring us to "claim all we're meant to be." Other songs in this collection also celebrate growing to all we can be in the divine image. "Holy Wisdom" and other biblical female divine names and images contribute to this spiritual growth. The first stanza of "She Lives and Moves Throughout the Earth" celebrates many of these names:

She lives within us and above, Holy Wisdom;
Her many names bring life and love, Holy Wisdom.
Hokmah and Sophia wise,
Mary Queen of earth and skies,
Ruah Spirit, El Shaddai,
Mother Hen, Sister Friend,
join Her new creation.

With Wisdom's ever-expanding view, we work together with people of diverse religious and spiritual traditions for justice and peace in our world. Interfaith collaboration is another theme in this song collection. When we take down divisive walls, we discover our common values and the power of our combined efforts to transform our world. In a world of wars and violence, oppression and brokenness, we can join together as sisters and brothers from many religious traditions to work for justice for all people and all creation. Many of the songs in this collection are appropriate for interfaith settings. Some specifically encourage the coming together of people from various traditions. "Gathered Here to Share Our Music," for example, sings of the blessing of "our diversity" and of "breaking walls and building bridges" to create community. "In Unity We Gather" rejoices in the gathering together of people from "many cultures, diverse in creed and race," concluding with this celebratory stanza:

In faith we are united, in hope and love set free;
through bridging our divisions we claim all we can be.
Together we envision a peaceful global home;
within Creative Mystery we find a deep Shalom.

Short Songs for Worship Services

Earth Transformed with Music! also includes short songs for various parts of worship services, such as calls to worship, invocations, responses to scripture, communion, and benedictions. These are inclusive, multigenerational songs that can be sung by congregations and/or choirs.

Several of these short pieces are incorporated into litanies as sung responses repeated throughout the litanies. Others are stand-alone responses to specific elements in the liturgy. Some of these short songs can be adapted for various parts of worship services. "For the Wisdom in the Word," for example, has several endings so that it can be sung as a call to worship, as a response to scripture or other worship readings, or as a benediction.

These short songs provide additional opportunities for everyone to participate in worship. Also, we hope that they, along with all the songs in this collection, will inspire communities and individuals to join in the creation of inclusive worship. This new song collection comes to you with the invitation to join in transforming earth through singing and creating inclusive songs that give birth to justice and peace.

Celebration, Liberation

1 Come, Sing of New Creation

Proverbs 3:17-18; Acts 2:17; 2 Corinthians 5:17

1. Come, sing of new cre - a - tion, un - fold - ing all our days,
2. Re - joice in past and pre - sent, in bless - ings through the years,
3. Our ded - i - cat - ed sis - ters in - spire our work each day,
4. Come, cel - e - brate all pi - o-neers who o - pen minds and doors,
as Ho - ly Wis - dom guides us in Her trans - form - ing ways.
in fu - ture sto - ries join - ing to make the Good News clear.
through words and ac - tions lead - ing to Wis - dom's peace - ful way.
as Ho - ly Wis - dom gives us Her pow - er ev - er - more.
Come, cel - e - brate our sis - ters who take down ev - ery wall,
Come, cel - e - brate our found - ers whose cour - age set us free,
Come, cel - e - brate the found - ers of new re - al - i - ty,
Our sons and daugh-ters preach - ing stir all to dream and dare,
through faith - ful ser - vice lead - ing in lib - er - at - ing all.
who blazed new paths to jus - tice, to full e - qual - i - ty.
who la - bor build - ing bridg - es, cre - at - ing syn - er - gy.
to co - cre - ate and nur - ture a world of lov - ing care.

Words: Jann Aldredge-Clanton
Music: *Wittenberg Gesangbuch*, 1784

ELLACOMBE
7.6.7.6 D

Renewing, Reforming the Church in Our Day 2

Luke 4:18-19; 2 Corinthians 5:17

1. Re - new - ing, re - form - ing the church in our day,
2. Our mis - sion re - claim - ing, we wit - ness a - new,
3. The Gos - pel ful - fill - ing, we free the op - pressed,
4. With grace still a - bound - ing, we change the world now;
for - ev - er trans - form - ing, we fol - low the Way,
to - geth - er pro - claim - ing a still wid - er view.
com - pas - sion in - still - ing, di - ver - si - ty blessed.
the Spir - it as - tound - ing is show - ing us how.
Good News for the poor, lib - er - a - tion for all;
With Spir - it - led call - ing to dream and to dare,
We pray that the Spir - it will make us all one,
As sis - ters and broth - ers, we join hand in hand
to - geth - er we an - swer the life - giv - ing call.
we la - bor for heal - ing, for peace ev - ery - where.
by bridg - ing di - vi - sions so Love's work is done.
to bring new cre - a - tion through - out ev - ery land.

Words: Jann Aldredge-Clanton
Music: Welsh hymn tune

ST. DENIO
11.11.11.11

3 Mary Magdalene Inspires Us

Luke 8:1-3; Matthew 5:9; Proverbs 1:20-23, 3:17; John 20:1-18; 1 Corinthians 1:24

Unison
1. Mar - y Mag - da - lene in - spires us on our jour - ney
2. Noth - ing can de - feat the mes - sage; Liv - ing Word will
3. Mar - y Mag - da - lene goes seek - ing just be - fore the
4. "Come and join the won-drous sto - ry, o - pen wide, af -
to new life; she and oth - er wom-en seek - ers find the Way to
nev - er die; hate and vio - lence can - not si - lence Ho - ly Wis-dom's
ris - ing sun, loy - al to the sa - cred mis - sion, first to see the
firm - ing all," Mar - y Mag - da - lene gives wit - ness to the all - in -
end the strife. These dis - ci - ples help the oth - ers,
ur - gent cry. Mar - y Mag - da - lene is listen - ing,
Ris - en One. As a - pos - tle to a - pos - tles,
clu - sive call. Word and Wis - dom guide us for - ward

Words: Jann Aldredge-Clanton
Music: Larry E. Schultz

SPIRIT DANCE
8.7.8.7 D

poco rit.
a tempo
giv - ing free - ly of their means, spread - ing Je - sus'
watch - ing, wait - ing all night long, stay - ing faith - ful
she runs quick - ly to pro - claim, "Come and see the
to a still ex - pand - ing view; when we wel - come
1, 2, 3.
peace - ful mes - sage, Bread of Life for all to
to the vi - sion, keep - ing hope a - live and
res - ur - rec - tion, mir - a - cle for all to
all with glad - ness, Christ - So - phi - a
4.
glean.
strong.
claim."
ri - ses new.

3a Mary Magdalene Inspires Us

Luke 8:1-3; Matthew 5:9; Proverbs 1:20-23, 3:17; John 20:1-18; 1 Corinthians 1:24

1. Mar - y Mag - da - lene in - spires us on our jour - ney to new life;
2. Noth - ing can de - feat the mes - sage; Liv - ing Word will nev - er die;
3. Mar - y Mag - da - lene goes seek - ing just be - fore the ris - ing sun,
4. "Come and join the won-drous sto - ry, o - pen wide, af - firm-ing all,"

she and oth - er wom - en seek - ers find the Way to end the strife.
hate and vio - lence can - not si - lence Ho - ly Wis - dom's ur - gent cry.
loy - al to the sa - cred mis - sion, first to see the Ris - en One.
Mar - y Mag - da - lene gives wit - ness to the all - in - clu - sive call.

These dis - ci - ples help the oth - ers, giv - ing free - ly of their means,
Mar - y Mag - da - lene is listen - ing, watch - ing, wait - ing all night long,
As a - pos - tle to a - pos - tles, she runs quick - ly to pro - claim,
Word and Wis - dom guide us for - ward to a still ex - pand - ing view;

spread - ing Je - sus' peace - ful mes - sage, Bread of Life for all to glean.
stay - ing faith - ful to the vi - sion, keep - ing hope a - live and strong.
"Come and see the res - ur - rec - tion, mir - a - cle for all to claim."
when we wel - come all with glad - ness, Christ-So - phi - a ris - es new.

Words: Jann Aldredge-Clanton
Music: attr. B.F. White; arr. Larry E. Schultz

BEACH SPRING
8.7.8.7 D

Miriam Shows Us Pathways to Freedom 4

Exodus 2:1-10, 15:20-21; Micah 6:4

Unison
1. Mir - i - am shows us path - ways to
2. Mir - i - am watch - es, cares for her
3. Mir - i - am danc - es, filled with e -
4. Work - ing for jus - tice takes all our
free - dom, sis - ter and proph - et, nur - tur - ing
broth - er, saves and pro - tects him for sa - cred
la - tion, joined with the wom - en, grate - ful and
pow - er; jour - neys to free - dom of - ten are
life; led by the Spir - it, guid - ed by
plan; sis - ter and broth - er joined with each
free, tam - bou - rines shak - ing with ju - bi -
long; filled with the Spir - it, dai - ly we
Wis - dom, Mir - i - am works for jus - tice to thrive.
oth - er, lead - ing the peo - ple to a new land.
la - tion, sing - ing of bless - ings, all that will be.
flow - er, joy - ful - ly sing - ing Mir - i - am's song.

Words: Jann Aldredge-Clanton
Music: Traditional Gaelic melody

BUNESSAN
5.5.5.4 D

5 We Gather in a Circle Here

Psalm 92:12-14; Proverbs 8:23; Acts 2:17

may be sung in a round

1. We gath - er in a cir - cle here
2. As fruit trees blos - som day and night,
3. We gath - er prais - ing ev - ery sage,
4. Wise wom - en lead the way to peace,

to cel - e - brate wise wom - en near;
wise wom - en bloom in beau - ty bright;
who grows in pow - er with each age;
that love and jus - tice may in - crease;

the im - age of So - phi - a wise,
they claim So - phi - a's grace and power,
So - phi - a Wis - dom gives new life,
they join So - phi - a, bold and free,

they bring us gifts to great - ly prize.
from age to age com - plete - ly flower.
all dreams and vi - sions to re - vive.
to birth a world more than we see.

Words: Jann Aldredge-Clanton
Music: Thomas Tallis

TALLIS' CANON
8.8.8.8 (LM)

We Work for Racial Justice Now 6

Genesis 1:27; Exodus 6:2-8

1. We work for ra - cial jus - tice now, for true e - qual - i - ty;
2. We work to stop in - jus - tice now, to end op - pres - sive ways;
3. O Sis - ter - Broth - er Spir - it, help us know Your breadth and height;
4. Come, Sis - ter - Broth - er Spir - it, come and heal our wound - ed past;
come, Sis - ter - Broth-er Spir - it, come and help us all be free.
come, Sis - ter - Broth-er Spir - it, come and guide to bet - ter days.
each cul-ture, ev - ery col - or shows Your im - age dark and bright.
to - geth - er we shall o - ver - come, and all be free at last.
We are claim-ing the prom - ised land; we are claim-ing the prom-ised land;
come, sis-ters, broth - ers, hand in hand; we are claim - ing the prom-ised land.

Words: Jann Aldredge-Clanton
Music: Matilda T. Durham; *Southern Harmony*, 1835

PROMISED LAND
8.6.8.6 (CM) with refrain

7 We Long for Change

Luke 4:18; Acts 2:17-18

1. We long for change, the wea - ry church re -
2. We long for church to give in - clu - sive
3. We work for change, the world - wide church re -
new - ing; we long for tak - ing down of ev - ery
bless - ing, af - firm - ing ev - ery gen - der, ev - ery
form - ing, the Good News bring - ing, set - ting cap - tives
wall, for o - pen hearts and minds to full - est
race, for church with o - pen doors, no one op -
free; we work for change, our words and deeds trans -

Words: Jann Aldredge-Clanton
Music: Traditional Irish melody

LONDONDERRY AIR
11.10.11.10 with refrain

view - ing the sa - cred worth and dig - ni - ty of all.
press - ing; we long for free - ly flow-ing love and grace.
form - ing, so ev - ery - one can be all we can be.
O Broth-er - Sis - ter Spir - it, give us pow - er to join with
You to change the church to - day, to bring new free-dom for all gifts to
flow - er, to show to all the world Your just and peace-ful way.

8 Follow Her Peaceful Ways

Proverbs 3:13-18, 1:20-23

Unison
1. Fol - low Her peace - ful ways; join Ho - ly Wis - dom, chang-ing the
2. Man - y through - out the world suf - fer from vio - lence, hun - ger, op-
3. Rise up to an - swer the call-ing of Wis - dom, work - ing to-
world with Her kind - ness and grace, bless-ing all cul - tures, all gen - ders and
pres - sion, and plun-dering of earth. Wis - dom cries out with a voice full of
geth - er for peace - ful re - forms. Come to the Tree of Life bloom - ing for-
rac - es, wel - com-ing all in Her lov - ing em - brace.
long-ing, "Join me in la - bor to bring peace to birth."
ev - er, fill - ing the world with Her love that trans - forms.
Harmony
Fol - low Her peace - ful ways! Fol - low Her peace - ful ways! Join Ho - ly

Words: Jann Aldredge-Clanton
Music: Larry E. Schultz

PEACEFUL WAYS
11.10.11.10 with refrain

Wis - dom to end all the strife. She gives us pow-er to
meet ev - ery chal-lenge; fol-low Her peace-ful ways, bring-ing new life.

Follow Her Peaceful Ways 8a

Proverbs 3:13-18, 1:20-23

1. Follow Her peaceful ways; join Holy Wisdom,
changing the world with Her kindness and grace,
blessing all cultures, all genders and races,
welcoming all in Her loving embrace. *(Refrain)*

2. Many throughout the world suffer from violence,
hunger, oppression, and plundering of earth.
Wisdom cries out with a voice full of longing,
"Join me in labor to bring peace to birth." *(Refrain)*

3. Rise up to answer the calling of Wisdom,
working together for peaceful reforms.
Come to the Tree of Life blooming forever,
filling the world with Her love that transforms. *(Refrain)*

Refrain: Follow Her peaceful ways! Follow Her peaceful ways!
Join Holy Wisdom to end all the strife.
She gives us power to meet every challenge;
follow Her peaceful ways, bringing new life.

Words: Jann Aldredge-Clanton
Music: William M. Runyan

FAITHFULNESS
11.10.11.10 with refrain

9 Our Lady Guadalupe

Psalm 139:12; Luke 1:26-55
1. Our La - dy Gua - da - lu - pe, so won - der - ful and wise,
2. Our La - dy Gua - da - lu - pe, the Queen of heaven and earth,
3. Our La - dy Gua - da - lu - pe, re - vive us day and night;
You o - pen hearts to vi - sion, to mar - vel - ous sur - prise.
re - stor - ing all cre - a - tion, You la - bor for re - birth.
Your im - age re - con - nects us, Your dark - ness and Your light.
A - wak - en all to sa - vor Your mir - a - cles each day,
Come now with Your new vi - sions, new won - ders to re - lease,
We join Your sa - cred mis - sion, em - bold - ened with Your power;
Your glo - rious rev - e - la - tions that show a heal - ing way.
in - spir - ing trans - for - ma - tion through jus - tice, love, and peace.
em - brac - ing all our tal - ents, to - geth - er we will flower.

Words: Jann Aldredge-Clanton
Music: Samuel S. Wesley

AURELIA
7.6.7.6 D

Longing to Be Free at Last

Exodus 16:1-12; Deuteronomy 34:1-4

1. Ru-ah Spir-it, il - lu-mine peace-ful ways; we are long-ing to be free at last; give us cour-age to end op - pres - sive days; we are long - ing to be free at last.
2. Ru-ah Spir-it, help all to end the strife; we are long-ing to be free at last; through the wil - der-ness, send Your bread of life; we are long - ing to be free at last.
3. Ru-ah Spir-it, re - veal the prom-ised land; we are long-ing to be free at last; guide us ev - er-more with Your power - ful hand; we are long - ing to be free at last.
Long - ing, long - ing, filled with a hope that holds us fast,
long - ing, long - ing, we are long-ing to be free at last.

Words: Jann Aldredge-Clanton
Music: A. J. Showalter

SHOWALTER
10.9.10.9 with refrain

11 Praise the Source of All Creation

Genesis 1:1-27, 31; Proverbs 3:13-18

1. Praise the Source of all cre - a - tion,
2. Man - y gen - ders, man - y rac - es,
3. Long have man - y been ex - clud - ed,
4. E - qual mar - riage, heal - ing, free - ing,
giv - ing life through - out the earth,
all re - flect Di - vin - i - ty;
judged and scorned by cus - tom's norms;
nur - tures bod - y, mind, and soul,
bless - ing ev - ery love re - la - tion,
man - y gifts and man - y grac - es
ev - ery - one will be in - clud - ed
re - af - firm - ing ev - ery be - ing,
fill - ing all with sa - cred worth.
help us be all we can be.
as we work to make re - forms.
all cre - at - ed good and whole.

Words: Jann Aldredge-Clanton
Music: Rowland H. Prichard

HYFRYDOL
8.7.8.7 D

Cel - e - brate all forms and col - ors,
Part - ners on this path of free - dom,
Let us end a - buse and vio - lence,
Come, re - joice and sing to - geth - er,
var - ied beau - ty ev - ery - where,
tak - ing down each sti - fling wall,
bring - ing jus - ticc ev - ery - where,
cel - e - brat - ing life and love;
streams of good - ness o - ver - flow - ing,
we will o - pen doors of wel - come,
join - ing Ho - ly Wis - dom's mis - sion,
praise the great Cre - a - tive Spir - it,
won - drous gifts for all to share.
bring - ing hope and joy to all.
help - ing all be free and fair.
liv - ing in us and a - bove.

12 Rejoicing, Reclaiming Our Life-Giving Call

Genesis 1:27, 31

1. Re - joic - ing, re - claim - ing our life - giv - ing call,
2. All gen - ders and rac - es we glad - ly af - firm,
3. The Spir - it re - veal - ing, we work for re - form,
4. Our pur - pose ful - fill - ing, we la - bor for life,
we join in pro - claim - ing the good - ness of all.
at all times and plac - es, our wel - come con - firm.
re - stor - ing and heal - ing with love that trans - forms.
com - pas - sion in - still - ing to end all the strife.
Our Mak - er has blessed ev - ery - one on the earth;
To those long ex - clud - ed by dog - ma and fear,
We cel - e - brate join - ing of bod - ies and souls
The Spir - it in - spires us to dream and to dare,
all im - age Di - vin - i - ty, share sa - cred worth.
we o - pen our doors so that all flour - ish here.
in var - ied re - la - tion-ships, e - qual and whole.
to bring lov - ing jus - tice and peace ev - ery - where.

Words: Jann Aldredge-Clanton
Music: Joseph Funk's *Genuine Church Music*, 1832

FOUNDATION
11.11.11.11

Celebrate This Congregation **13**

Luke 4:18; 1 Corinthians 12:4-31; Revelation 21:1-6

1. Cel-e-brate this con-gre-ga-tion, mov-ing bold-ly through the years,
2. All are wel-comed at our ta-ble, all af-firmed in lov-ing care;
3. Sis-ter-Broth-er Spir-it guides us, show-ing true e-qual-i-ty;

feed-ing bod-y, mind, and spir-it, bring-ing jus-tice far and near.
heal-ing pain, re-stor-ing pow-er, we u-nite to dream and dare.
lib-er-at-ing sons and daugh-ters, we af-firm di-ver-si-ty.

Var-ied gifts and var-ied per-sons nour-ish true com-mu-ni-ty;
Ho-ly Wis-dom guides our mis-sion, bring-ing Good News un-to all;
Man-y rac-es, man-y gen-ders, all cre-ate a full-er view;

with our Mak-er's grace and pow-er, we are set-ting cap-tives free.
join-ing hands for peace and jus-tice, we ful-fill our sa-cred call.
join to-geth-er, now re-joic-ing, cel-e-brat-ing life a-new.

Words: Jann Aldredge-Clanton
Music: John Zundel

BEECHER
8.7.8.7 D

Comfort, Power

14 All Day and Night Shekhinah* Guides Us

Exodus 40:34-38, 29:45

1. All day and night She - khi - nah guides us; with - in our spir - its
2. Al - ways She - khi - nah feels our sor - row, giv - ing us com - fort
3. Dai - ly She - khi - nah gives us pow - er, help-ing us claim our
She a - bides. Kind-ness and wis - dom deep in - side us,
through the pain; shar - ing our grief now and to - mor-row,
sa - cred worth; all of our gifts will ful - ly flow - er,
She keeps our spir - its o - pen wide; so we af - firm and
She gives us grace to ease the strain. All of our fears we
join - ing to bring new life to birth. Dwell-ing in Her we're
wel - come all, join - ing with Her to take down walls.
can re - lease; She gives us cour - age, hope, and peace.
whole and free, dream - ing of more than we can see.

Words: Jann Aldredge-Clanton
Music: Georg Neumark

**Shekhinah* is a feminine Hebrew word translated "dwelling" or "settling," and is used to denote the dwelling presence of God and/or the glory of God.

NEUMARK
9.8.9.8.8.8

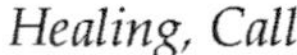

Where She Dwells, There Is Love 15

1 John 4:16

1. The Spir - it in - vites us to fol - low Her way, to
2. Where jus - tice in - creas - es, where peace work is done, Her
3. The Spir - it in - spires us to join Her each day; She

find Her at work ev - ery - where; we o - pen our hearts to Her
Love reach - es ful - ly to all; She wel - comes, af - firms, and in -
calls from with - in and a - bove; we find Her trans - form - ing, com -

heal - ing each day, and dis - cov - er Her kind - ness to share.
cludes ev - ery - one, as we an - swer Her life - giv - ing call.
pas - sion - ate way, and be - come Her di - vine, won - drous Love.

Where She dwells, there is Love;
Where She dwells, there is
Love;

where She dwells, where She dwells, there is Love.

Words: Jann Aldredge-Clanton
Music: Philip P. Bliss

VILLE DU HAVRE
11.8.11.9 with refrain

16 Where Are Liberty and Justice?

Amos 4:1, 5:11-12, 24; Proverbs 1:20-23, 3:13-18

1. Where are lib - er - ty and jus - tice
2. Now the rich are grow - ing rich - er,
3. How un - just that some make mil - lions,
4. Ho - ly Wis - dom, send us for - ward,
when so man - y live in need?
while the poor cry in dis - tress;
crush - ing oth - ers with their greed,
work - ing for e - qual - i - ty,
Let us rise to car - ing ac - tion,
heads of cor - po - ra - tions flour - ish,
bas - ic rights of work - ers flaunt - ing,
ec - o - nom - ic fair - ness bring - ing,
show - ing faith and love through deeds.
while the poor have less and less.
nev - er hear - ing those in need.
mak - ing dreams re - al - i - ty.

Words: Jann Aldredge-Clanton
Music: Thomas John Williams

EBENEZER
8.7.8.7 D

3
Ho - ly Wis - dom, give us cour - age;
Mil - lions suf - fer un - em - ploy - ment;
Ho - ly Wis - dom, come to help us;
As we join with those who suf - fer,
help us be Your proph - ets bold,
man - y more are un - der - paid;
give us pow - er to u - nite,
fill us with Your lov - ing care;
join - ing You to end op - pres - sion,
give us pow - er, Ho - ly Wis - dom,
mov - ing hearts and chang - ing sys - tems,
may we take Your peace - ful path - ways,
truth and fair - ness to up - hold.
so that chang - es can be made.
join - ing hands to work for right.
bring - ing jus - tice ev - ery - where.

Lament, Social Justice

17 We Hear the Cries of Millions

Amos 5:11-12, 21-24
1. We hear the cries of mil - lions, weighed down with stress and strain;
2. Now jobs are get - ting scarc - er, while cor - po - ra - tions thrive;
3. Join hands for jobs with jus - tice, with work - ers' rights en - sured,
4. Now let us work to - geth - er to bring e - qual - i - ty,
the rich are grow - ing rich - er; the poor cry out in pain.
the un - em - ployed are strug - gling to keep their hope a - live.
with safe and fair con - di - tions, health care for all se - cured.
so all are ful - ly nour - ished to be all we can be.
Come, Sis - ter - Broth - er Spir - it, and help us all u - nite,
Come, Broth - er - Sis - ter Spir - it, and guide us to be fair,
Come, Sis - ter - Broth - er Spir - it, and fill us with Your power;
Let jus - tice roll like wa - ters, like ev - er - flow - ing streams
to join in lov - ing - kind - ness and faith to work for right.
to change op - pres - sive sys - tems so ev - ery - one will share.
in - spire our words and ac - tions in this most ur - gent hour.
come, Broth - er - Sis - ter Spir - it, a - wak - en hopes and dreams.

Words: Jann Aldredge-Clanton
Music: Hans Leo Hassler; harm. J. S. Bach

PASSION CHORALE
7.6.7.6 D

Rise Up and Shout

Proverbs 1:20-23, 3:13-18; Luke 4:18

1. When we look all a - round, un - em - ploy - ment a - bounds, and we're filled with dis - tress, fear, and doubt. Then we hear Wis - dom say, "We can show a new way." And She leads us to rise and speak out.
2. There are mil - lions in need, crushed by oth - ers with greed, who a - buse and op - press with their clout. Wis - dom calls us to go, and Her jus - tice to show, and She leads us with love to speak out.
3. There'll be fair - ness and peace; work - ers' rights will in - crease when we wake up and hear Wis - dom shout. Let us come and u - nite, work - ing dai - ly for right; join to - geth - er to rise and speak out.
Rise up and shout, for it's time to speak out; let us cry out for jus - tice; let us rise and speak out.

Words: Jann Aldredge-Clanton
Music: Daniel B. Towner

TRUST AND OBEY
Irregular

19 Join Together, Work for Justice

Proverbs 3:13-18

1. Join to-geth-er, work for jus-tice, car-ing for all work-ers' plights,
2. Come to-geth-er now for ac-tion; male and fe-male all u-nite;
3. Join to-geth-er now in cir-cles, sa-cred space for ev-ery voice,

chang-ing sti-fling sex-ist cus-toms; wom-en's rights are hu-man rights;
join-ing hands for jobs with jus-tice, la-bor for all hu-man rights.
work-ing for a world of jus-tice, e-qual rights and e-qual choice.

call for e-qual pay and ac-cess; wom-en's rights are work-ers' rights
Ho-ly Wis-dom guides us for-ward, shows new pat-terns to ar-range
Shar-ing lib-er-at-ing sto-ries, we cre-ate the world a-new;

Ho-ly Wis-dom guides our la-bor, giv-ing strength all day and night.
fol-low Her trans-form-ing path-ways, mak-ing peace, in-spir-ing change.
Ho-ly Wis-dom guides our vi-sion, giv-ing all Her glo-rious view.

Words: Jann Aldredge-Clanton
Music: Franz Joseph Haydn

AUSTRIAN HYMN
8.7.8.7 D

All Who Labor Through Day and Night 20

Galatians 5:22, 25
Unison
1. All who labor through day and night, all who labor through day and night, come together; work for justice, joined with the Spirit of truth and right.
2. In our labor for workers' rights, in our labor for workers' rights, we will challenge greedy powers, joined with the Spirit who feels our plight.
3. In our labor we feel the call; in our labor we feel the call; we unite now, bringing justice, joined with the Spirit within us all.
4. By our labor we take down walls; by our labor we take down walls; we unite now, building bridges, joined with the Spirit within us all.
Words: Jann Aldredge-Clanton
Music: African-American spiritual
Words © 2014 Jann Aldredge-Clanton.
SOJOURNER
8.8.8.9

Epiphany, Social Justice

21 A Stranger, Starving on the Street

Matthew 25:35-40; Luke 24:13-35

1. A stran - ger, starv - ing on the street, from
2. She moves in - to our sa - cred space, where,
3. With o - pened eyes and grate - ful hearts, im -
4. In - spired by her, trans - formed and freed, com -
trav - el, tired and sore, has found a place to
from the ta - ble spread, she gives to us the
ag - i - na - tions stirred through joy - ful song, cre -
pelled be - yond our door, we'll go in - to the
rest her feet be - side our church - 's door.
cup of grace, for us breaks liv - ing bread.
a - tive arts, and thought - pro - vok - ing word,
cit - y street a - mong the starv - ing poor.

Words: Larry E. Schultz

Music: English Traditional; *English Country Songs*, 1893

KINGSFOLD
8.6.8.6 D (CMD)

We bring her wa - ter, give her food, then
As - ton - ished as we take and taste, our
we cel - e - brate the nour - ish - ment she
A - wak - ened to each per - son's need of
of - fer swift good - byes; yet, with her hun - ger
cloud - ed sight turns clear: this hun - gry one dis -
of - fers in this meal – an un - ex - pect - ed
bod - y, soul and mind, we'll strength - en, com - fort,
un - sub - dued, she takes us by sur - prise:
missed in haste is Christ who feeds us here!
sac - ra - ment to bless, re - new and heal.
hum - bly feed, and be the Christ they find!

(Opt. Tenor G# in final chord of Stanza 4)

Call

22 Who Will Help All Those in Need?

Proverbs 3:17-18, 4:10-18; Luke 4:18

1. Who will help all those in need, strug - gling in a world of greed? Where is good news for the poor? Who will o - pen free - dom's door? We will an - swer Wis - dom's call.
2. Who em - pow - ers ev - ery race, cel - e - brates each gift and grace? Who will keep the dream a - live, help - ing ev - ery - one to thrive? We will an - swer Wis - dom's call.
3. Who af - firms each gen - der's worth, brings e - qual - i - ty to birth? Who will work for lib - er - ty, help - ing all be fair and free? We will an - swer Wis - dom's call.
4. Ho - ly Wis - dom is the Way, Truth, and Life for all to - day. On Her peace - ful paths we go, lov - ing - kind - ness dai - ly show. We will an - swer Wis - dom's call.

Words: Jann Aldredge-Clanton
Music: César Malan

HENDON
7.7.7.7.7

Praise the Source of Every Blessing 23

Psalm 104:10-25; Proverbs 3:17-18; Isaiah 35:1-10

1. Praise the Source of ev - ery bless - ing, bring-ing good-ness
2. Praise the Ho - ly Way of jus - tice, lead - ing us to
3. Praise the Well of Ho - ly Wis - dom, flow - ing deep with -
4. Praise the great Cre - a - tive Spir - it, birth - ing beau - ty
to the Earth, lov - ing ev - ery liv - ing be - ing,
work for right; join to heal all wound - ed na - ture,
in our souls, guid - ing us to save cre - a - tion,
ev - ery - where, mov - ing us to lov - ing ac - tion,
fill - ing all with sa - cred worth. Al - le - lu - ia!
frac - tured, poi - soned, scarred with blight. Voic - es raised to
care - less ac - tions to con - trol. Still con - serv - ing,
that Her treas - ures all may share. Al - le - lu - ia!
Al - le - lu - ia! Ra - diant life She brings to birth.
stop de - struc - tion, we will la - bor day and night.
still pro - tect - ing, we will make Earth safe and whole.
Al - le - lu - ia! Earth calls for our ten - der care.

Words: Jann Aldredge-Clanton
Music: John Goss

LAUDA ANIMA
8.7.8.7.8.7

24 O Earth, We Hear Your Cries of Pain

Genesis 1:29-31; Psalm 104:5-30
1. O Earth, we hear your cries of pain, your cries of des - o - la - tion;
2. O Earth, we hear you call - ing us to work for con - ser - va - tion,
3. We thank you, Earth, for all your gifts that show your grace and pow-er,
we join to heal your man - y wounds, to bring your res - to - ra - tion.
to nur - ture life in ev - ery form, to care for all cre - a - tion.
your fra - grant fruit, your rip-ened grain, your gold - en trees and flow-ers.
Pol - lut - ed air and poi-soned seas en - dan - ger all the liv - ing;
By clean-ing wa - ter, air, and land, we join to work for heal-ing;
We join to save your love - ly life, to work for trans - for - ma - tion,
if greed - y hands use up your wealth, you can - not keep on giv - ing.
each day you bring new life to birth, your beau - ty still re - veal-ing.
to change de-struc-tive sys - tems now, to start a ref - or - ma - tion.

Words: Jann Aldredge-Clanton
Music: Robert Lowry

ENDLESS SONG
8.7.8.7 D

Ruah, the Spirit, Dwells 25

Isaiah 35:1-7

1. Ru - ah, the Spir - it, dwells in ev - ery liv - ing cell
2. Poi - soned and scarred by greed, Earth now cries out in need,
3. Streams in the de - sert flow, gar - dens of beau - ty grow
4. Ru - ah cre - ates a - new, and ev - ery life im - bues
She brings to birth. Join in Her car - ing ways,
seek - ing re - birth. Ru - ah, the Spir - it, hears
by Ru - ah's hand. Still Her cre - a - tive power
with sa - cred worth. Join to con - serve Her gifts,
work - ing for bet - ter days; join Her to
and brings Her heal - ing near, send - ing Her
brings na - ture's gifts to flower, call - ing us
join now with ac - tion swift, and all our
loud - ly say, "Help save the Earth."
mes - sage clear, "Help save the Earth."
ev - ery hour, "Help save the land."
voic - es lift, "Help save the Earth."

Words: Jann Aldredge-Clanton
Music: *Thesaurus Musicus,* 1744

AMERICA
6.6.4.6.6.6.4

26 Sophia Wisdom Shows the Way

Proverbs 3:17-18

1. So - phi - a Wis - dom shows the way to lib - er - at - ing life,
2. The land is scarred and frac - tured deep; pol - lu - tion fills the air,
3. So - phi - a Wis - dom still cre - ates new beau - ty ev - ery day,
to car - ing for cre - a - tion now, so Earth will long sur - vive.
and poi-soned o - ceans threat - en life; it's time to show we care.
the gold - en trees, the danc - ing deer, the flow - ers' wild dis - play.
A - wake to work and ad - vo-cate to save Earth's treas - ures rare,
So - phi - a Wis - dom calls to us to stop de - struc - tive ways,
Come, join So - phi - a, nur - tur - ing Her pre - cious gifts for all;
pro - tect - ing all the liv - ing ones, all na - ture ev - ery - where.
to work with Her in sav - ing life, to act with-out de - lay.
con - serv - ing life in ev - ery form ful - fills our sa - cred call.

Words: Jann Aldredge-Clanton
Music: Samuel A. Ward

MATERNA
8.6.8.6.D (CMD)

Come, Join with the Children

Genesis 1

1. Come, join with the chil - dren; come, join, one and all,
to care for cre - a - tion, ful - fill - ing our call;
come, join Ru - ah Spir - it in giv - ing new birth,
and la - bor to - geth - er in nur - tur - ing Earth.

2. We glad - ly re - cy - cle and joy - ful - ly share,
and call on the mak - ers of laws to be fair,
to join Ru - ah Spir - it in car - ing for life,
pro - tect - ing, con - serv - ing, so all will sur - vive.

3. Come, join with all ag - es to care for the Earth,
to save na - ture's treas - ures, to val - ue their worth;
come, join Ru - ah Spir - it in car - ing each day;
She gives us the wis - dom to fol - low Her way.

Words: Jann Aldredge-Clanton
Music: Johann A. P. Schulz

SCHULZ
6.5.6.5 D

28 Holy Wisdom Still Is Calling

Proverbs 1:20-23, 3:17-18; Isaiah 65:17-25

1. Ho-ly Wis-dom still is call-ing, "Who will take my paths of peace?"
2. Ho-ly Wis-dom still is call-ing, "Who will help my world to mend,
3. Ho-ly Wis-dom still is call-ing, "Who will work to end the strife?"

Long Her ur-gent cry has sound-ed, "When will all the vio-lence cease?"
work to stop the wars of na-tions and do-mes-tic vio-lence end?"
Long Her pa-tient call has sound-ed, "Who will nur-ture all of life?"

Wars in man-y lands are rag-ing, and on man-y cit-y streets;
We will join in Wis-dom's mis-sion, bring-ing heal-ing ev-ery-where,
We will glad-ly an-swer Wis-dom, work with Her for peace on earth,

"Who will work to stop the fight-ing?" Ho-ly Wis-dom still en-treats.
chang-ing all op-pres-sive sys-tems as with Her we dream and dare.
take Her paths of love and jus-tice, new cre-a-tion now to birth.

Words: Jann Aldredge-Clanton
Music: attr. Wolfgang Amadeus Mozart

ELLESDIE
8.7.8.7 D

Sister Wisdom, Come to Guide Us 29

Proverbs 3:13-18, 7:4

1. Sis - ter Wis - dom, come to guide us on Your heal - ing paths of peace;
2. Wis - dom, You are friend and sis - ter, close com - pan - ion on our way;
3. Sis - ter Wis - dom, liv - ing in us, may we hear Your lov - ing call;
give us cour - age for each chal - lenge, that Your jus - tice may in - crease.
Your sup - port - ive love sus - tains us, giv - ing strength for ev - ery day.
with Your lib - er - at - ing pow - er, we take down each sti - fling wall.
Joined with You we dream and dare, all Your bless - ings free - ly share.
Through each strug - gle that we face, You bring com - fort, hope, and grace.
Show us all Your glo - rious view, earth trans - formed, cre - a - tion new.

Words: Jann Aldredge-Clanton
Music: Henry J. Gauntlett

IRBY
8.7.8.7.7.7

30 Hope Springs Anew

Proverbs 3:17-18; Isaiah 35:1-10, 55:12-13, 58:6-8

1. Hope springs a - new through - out the earth,
2. Love ris - es up to end the strife,
3. Peace flows with - in us ev - ery day,
4. Joy blos - soms free - ly through each land,
as Ho - ly Wis - dom brings new birth.
as Ho - ly Wis - dom brings new life.
as Ho - ly Wis - dom shows the way.
when touched by Wis - dom's ten - der hand.
She guides us on Her paths of peace,
She gives us grace to wel - come all,
She bless - es those who hold Her fast,
She leads to sa - cred heal - ing springs,
that lov - ing - kind - ness will in - crease.
to take down each di - vid - ing wall.
that we may all be free at last.
as all cre - a - tion claps and sings.

Words: Jann Aldredge-Clanton
Music: Thomas Williams' *Psalmodia Evangelica*, 1789

TRURO
8.8.8.8 (LM)

Shekhinah* Dwells Within Our Hearts 31

Exodus 29:45, 40:34-38

1. She - khi - nah dwells with - in our hearts, in -
2. She - khi - nah gives us all we need to
3. She - khi - nah shines in all the earth through
spir - ing peace - ful ways. She guides our jour - ney,
keep our cour - age strong. Her wis - dom guides our
gifts so full and fair. She shows us ways to
calms our fears, through - out the nights and days. She
jus - tice work on paths so hard and long. She
nur - ture life with ten - der lov - ing care. To -
helps us keep our hope a - live, and with us al - ways stays.
gives us pow - er, love, and grace, and lifts our hearts with song.
geth - er let us cel - e - brate Her glo - ry ev - ery - where.

Words: Jann Aldredge-Clanton

Music: attr. Elkanah Kelsay Dare; Wyeth's *Repository of Sacred Music, Part Second*, 1813

MORNING SONG
8.6.8.6.8.6

**Shekhinah* is a feminine Hebrew word translated "dwelling" or "settling," and is used to denote the dwelling presence of God and/or the glory of God.

32 Come, Mother Eagle, Show the Way

Deuteronomy 32:11-12; 2 Corinthians 5:17

3/4
1. Come, Moth - er Ea - gle, show the way to
2. Come, Moth - er Ea - gle, stir us now to
3. Come, Moth - er Ea - gle, give us flight to
4. Come, Moth - er Ea - gle, lift us all to
3
streams of kind - ness flow - ing; we
leave con - fin - ing plac - es, to
glo - rious rev - e - la - tions; il -
soar with You in dar - ing, to
long to live in peace - ful lands, where
rise to wel - come ev - ery - one, all
lu - mine ways to change our world, to
co - cre - ate a world of peace, of
love is ev - er grow - ing.
gen - ders, forms, and rac - es.
join in new cre - a - tion.
beau - ty, joy, and shar - ing.

Words: Jann Aldredge-Clanton
Music: Irish melody

ST. COLUMBA
8.7.8.7

Praise Sophia, Holy Wisdom 33

Exodus 40:34-38; Psalm 22:9-10; Proverbs 3:17-18; Isaiah 66:13; John 15:15

1. Praise So - phi - a, Ho - ly Wis-dom; praise Her man-y names and forms,
2. Come, re - joice in past and pre - sent min - is - try of lov - ing care,
3. Cel - e - brate pro - phet - ic mis - sion, bring - ing full e - qual - i - ty,
4. Cel - e - brate pro - phet - ic vi - sion, lead - ing to a peace - ful day,

Mid - wife, Friend, She - khi - nah, Moth - er, giv - ing power to make re - forms.
o - pening doors, af - firm - ing tal - ents, stir - ring all to dream and dare.
with the ris - en Christ-So - phi - a, mak - ing hope re - al - i - ty.
show - ing paths of Ho - ly Wis - dom, She Who Is the liv - ing Way.

Cel - e - brate Her church and proph - ets, bring - ing change for man - y years,
Cel - e - brate pro - phet - ic voice for chang - ing church and sys - tems wide,
Come, em - brace di - vine a - bun - dance, ho - ly nur - ture for all earth,
Come, re - joice in gifts and grac - es, flow - ing from Her sa - cred call,

show - ing all in - clu - sive jus - tice, spread - ing bless - ings far and near.
call - ing us to free all peo - ple with our lib - er - at - ing Guide.
through our lan - guage, art, and ac - tions, new cre - a - tion now to birth.
streams of beau - ty, love, and jus - tice, bring - ing life a - new to all.

Words: Jann Aldredge-Clanton
Music: Ludwig van Beethoven

HYMN TO JOY
8.7.8.7 D

34 She Lives and Moves Throughout the Earth

Proverbs 1:20-23, 3:17-18

1. She lives with - in us and a - bove, Ho - ly Wis - dom; Her man - y names bring life and love, Ho-ly Wis - dom. Hok-mah and So - phi - a wise, Mar - y Queen of earth and skies, Ru - ah Spir - it, El Shad-dai, Moth - er Hen, Sis - ter Friend, join Her new cre - a - tion.
2. She preach - es through Her proph-ets bold, Ho - ly Wis - dom; Her voice calls out to young and old, Ho-ly Wis - dom. A - mos, Mi - cah, Mag - da - lene, Es - ther, and I - sa - iah dream, show-ing paths we have not seen, paths of peace, vio-lence ceased; join Her new cre - a - tion.
3. She comes to sound her peace-ful call, Ho - ly Wis - dom; She is a Tree of Life for all, Ho-ly Wis - dom. Bless-ing those who hold Her fast, blend - ing fu - ture, pre - sent, past, help - ing all be free at last, Wis - dom-Word now is heard; join Her new cre - a - tion.

Words: Jann Aldredge-Clanton

Music: *Chorale melodien zum heiligen Gesange*, 1808

SALVE REGINA COELITUM
8.4.8.4.7.7.7.6.6

Come Rejoicing, Celebrating Life Together 35

Proverbs 3:17-18; 2 Corinthians 5:17

1. Come re - joic - ing, cel - e - brat - ing life to - geth - er through the years,
2. Learn-ing, grow-ing here to-geth - er, we cre - ate the church a - new,
3. Cel - e - brate the Ho - ly Mys - tery, deep with - in us and a - bove,
be - ing church in man - y plac - es, joined in mis - sion far and near.
still re - form - ing and trans-form - ing, lead - ing to a wid - er view.
giv - ing pow - er for each chal-lenge, fill - ing all with hope and love.
Ho - ly Wis - dom still is guid-ing, show - ing all Her paths of peace;
Sis - ter - Broth - er Spir - it guid-ing, we claim all we're meant to be,
Past and pre - sent flow to - geth-er, streams of bless - ing, full and free;
like the trees in full - est blos - som, all our tal - ents will in - crease.
join - ing in the new cre - a - tion far be - yond all we can see.
fu - ture vi - sions guide us for - ward, mak-ing dreams re - al - i - ty.

Words: Jann Aldredge-Clanton
Music: Wyeth's *Repository of Sacred Music, Part Second,* 1813

NETTLETON
8.7.8.7 D

Miracle

36 The Sacred Realm Is Like the Yeast

Luke 13:20-21

1. The sa - cred realm is like the yeast a Wom - an stirs in flour;
2. The leav - en that the Wom - an used was hat - ed, cast a - way,
3. The Bak - er Wom - an bless - es all, in - clud - ing last and least;
then wait - ing for the ris - ing, She watch - es hour by hour.
but hid - den in Her power - ful hands, a mir - a - cle dis - plays.
by join - ing Her cre - a - tive work, we all be - come the yeast.
The Bak - er Wom - an, strong and good, cre - ates the sa - vory bread;
The small - est bit of yeast be - comes a feast for ev - ery - one,
Our small - est acts of love and peace rise up to fill the earth,
She works to make up man - y loaves, so ev - ery - one is fed.
a - bun - dant good - ness fill - ing earth from dawn to set - ting sun.
trans - form - ing all with Bread of Life: "Take, eat, and taste re - birth."

Words: Jann Aldredge-Clanton
Music: Traditional Irish melody

CLONMEL
8.6.8.6 D (CMD)

Holy, Wondrous Mystery, Birthing All Creation 37

Genesis 1; Isaiah 45:3

1. Ho - ly, won-drous Mys - tery, birth - ing all cre - a - tion,
2. Ho - ly, won-drous Mys - tery, One in all things dwell - ing,
3. Ho - ly, won-drous Mys - tery, dark - ness mag - ni - fies You;
4. Ho - ly, won-drous Mys - tery, birth - ing all cre - a - tion,
ev - ery day Your songs a - rise from na - ture's har - mo - ny;
ev - ery - where in ev - ery - one You bring di - vin - i - ty;
in the dark - ened depths of soil You root and sprout and thrive;
all Your works re - sound in praise from earth and sky and sea;
ho - ly, won-drous Mys - tery, Breath of our for - ma - tion,
ho - ly, sa - cred Pres - ence, lov - ing and com - pel - ling,
ho - ly, spa - cious Dark - ness, moon and sun shine through You;
ho - ly, won-drous Mys - tery, glo - rious Rev - e - la - tion,
Source of all Life through - out in - fin - i - ty.
liv - ing and mov - ing through e - ter - ni - ty.
stars on Your can - vas bring the skies to life.
Song of all Life through - out in - fin - i - ty!

Words: Larry E. Schultz & Jann Aldredge-Clanton
Music: John Bacchus Dykes

NICAEA
Irregular

Freedom, Power

38 Our Great Creator Lives in All

Proverbs 3:17; Isaiah 55:12-13; John 10:34

1. Our great Creator lives in all
throughout the world in every form.
We feel Her gentle, loving call
to work with Her to bring reform.

2. With Her we work to transform hearts,
that all abuse and violence cease.
She gives us wisdom to impart,
to help the captives find release.

3. Her many names help us to know
the truth of our Divinity.
Within Her life we daily flow,
enlivened with new energy.

4. How marvelous that all are one,
the sacred image of Her Love.
All nature sings of wonders done,
Her glory in us and above.

Words: Jann Aldredge-Clanton
Music: Thomas Campbell

SAGINA
8.8.8.8.8.8 with refrain

She guides us on Her paths of peace, that love and jus - tice will in - crease.
With Her we join to spread Good News, the mes - sage of Her wid - er view.
Ru - ah, She - khi - nah, Mar - y Queen, She comes in ways more than we've seen.
Her beau - ty shines through - out the earth; She brings a - bun - dant life to birth.
Her pow - er sets all peo - ple free to be all we are meant to be.
Her pow - er sets all peo - ple free to be all we

39 In Unity We Gather

Psalm 133:1; Proverbs 3:17; Isaiah 55:12; 1 Corinthians 13:13

1. In u - ni - ty we gath - er, re - joic - ing in this place;
2. We cel - e - brate our one - ness with - in di - ver - si - ty,
3. Through shar - ing of our mu - sic we build com - mu - ni - ty;
4. In faith we are u - nit - ed, in hope and love set free;
we come from man - y cul - tures, di - verse in creed and race.
our var - ied voic - es join - ing, cre - at - ing har - mo - ny.
the great Cre - a - tive Spir - it in - spires our syn - er - gy.
through bridg - ing our di - vi - sions we claim all we can be.
Our voic - es blend to - geth - er to praise Cre - a - tive Love,
To - geth - er in the mu - sic all tal - ents will in - crease,
The clap - ping trees and riv - ers are join - ing in our praise,
To - geth - er we en - vi - sion a peace - ful glob - al home;
to sing of beau - ty dwell - ing a - mong us and a - bove.
and with Cre - a - tive Wis - dom we o - pen paths of peace.
and all cre - a - tion vi - brates with songs of joy we raise.
with - in Cre - a - tive Mys - tery we find a deep Sha - lom.

Words: Jann Aldredge-Clanton
Music: Henry T. Smart

LANCASHIRE
7.6.7.6 D

We Praise the Source of Life

Genesis 1:1-2; Psalm 133:1; 1 John 4:16-21

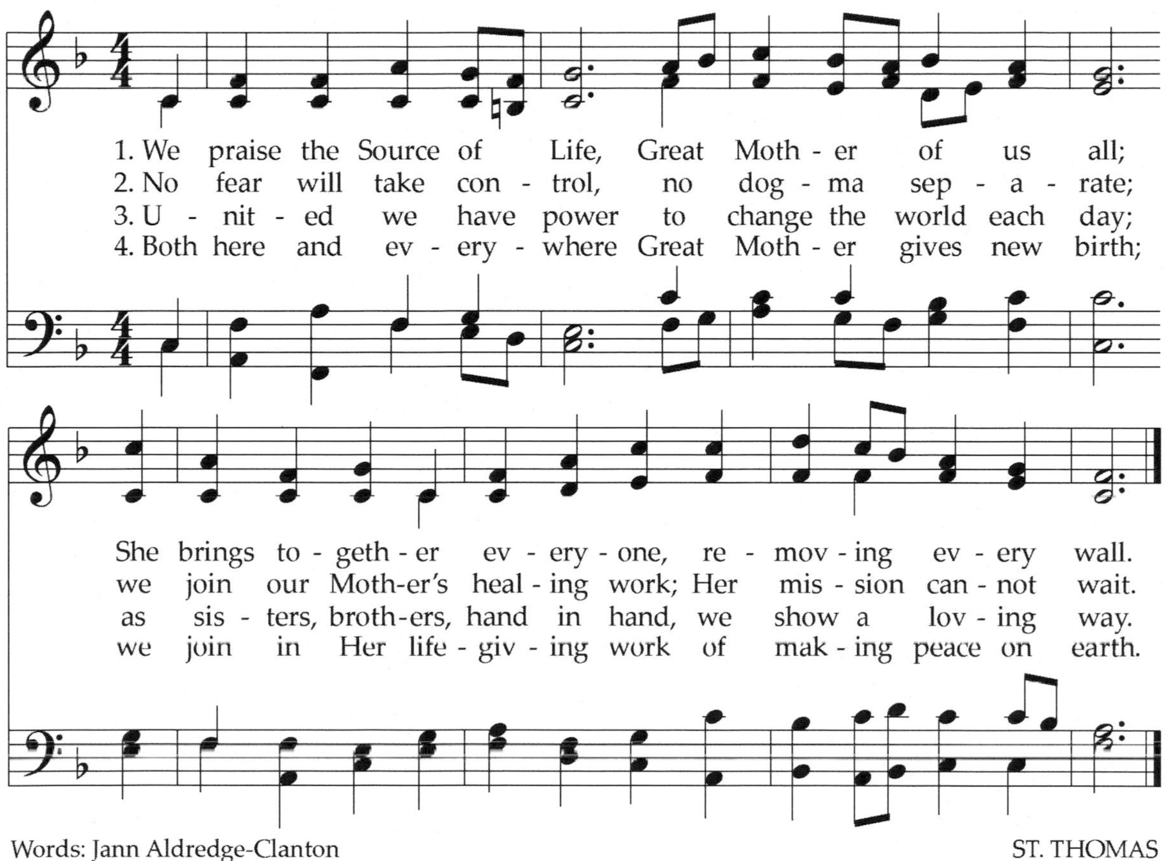
1. We praise the Source of Life, Great Moth - er of us all;
2. No fear will take con - trol, no dog - ma sep - a - rate;
3. U - nit - ed we have power to change the world each day;
4. Both here and ev - ery - where Great Moth - er gives new birth;
She brings to - geth - er ev - ery - one, re - mov - ing ev - ery wall.
we join our Moth-er's heal - ing work; Her mis - sion can - not wait.
as sis - ters, broth-ers, hand in hand, we show a lov - ing way.
we join in Her life - giv - ing work of mak - ing peace on earth.

Words: Jann Aldredge-Clanton
Music: Aaron Williams

ST. THOMAS
6.6.8.6 (SM)

41 Gathered Here to Share Our Music

Galatians 5:22; 2 Corinthians 5:17

1. Gath - ered here to share our mu - sic, gath - ered here in
2. Songs of faith and hope u - nite us; songs of heal - ing
3. Learn - ing, grow - ing here to - geth - er, var - ied gifts en -
4. Shar - ing songs from man - y plac - es, mov - ing in a
u - ni - ty, we have come from var - ied cul - tures,
set us free; break - ing walls and build - ing bridg - es,
rich - ing all, we ex - plore the power of mu - sic,
cir - cle wide, we dis - cov - er worlds of beau - ty,
blessed by our di - ver - si - ty.
we cre - ate com - mu - ni - ty.
faith - ful to our sa - cred call.
with our lib - er - at - ing Guide.

Words: Jann Aldredge-Clanton
Music: Dutch melody

IN BABILONE
8.7.8.7 D

Blend - ing man - y gifts and voic - es, sing - ing peace for
With the sa - cred Spir - it dwell - ing deep in us and
Like the man - y notes con - verg - ing, blend - ing in a
As we join the cos - mic cho - rus, hope springs up, sur -
all the earth, we will join the Spir - it's la - bor,
ev - ery - where, we are filled with lov - ing - kind - ness,
sym - pho - ny, all our cul - tures, all tra - di - tions
prise a - bounds; all cre - a - tion now is sing - ing,
giv - ing new cre - a - tion birth.
peace and joy for all to share.
join in grace - filled har - mo - ny.
earth trans - formed with joy re - sounds.

Community, Freedom

42 From Wisdom Emerging

Galatians 3:28; 1 John 4:16

Unison
1. From Wis - dom e - merg - ing, we
2. Faith's jour - ney re - claim - ing, we
3. For - ev - er ex - plor - ing, we
4. The fu - ture pro - gress - ing, we
fash - ion a space for peo - ple con - verg - ing in
blaze a new trail with oth - ers, ex - claim - ing: "Let
seek to learn more of Wis - dom's out - pour - ing, of
move through its change, old sys - tems re - dress - ing, new
safe - ty and grace, to shel - ter the free - dom of
jus - tice pre - vail!" Re - ject - ing worn paths that op -
Love's o - pen door. A - mazed at the mys - teries and
pat - terns ar - range; pro - tect - ing all free - doms with

Words and Music: Larry E. Schultz

VESTA
11.11.11.11

one and of all in Love with - out bor - der or
press and mis - lead, we walk in com - mu - ni - ty,
grac - es we find, we joy - ful - ly share them with
ev - ery new choice, we fol - low the Spir - it and
1, 2, 3.
4.
bound - ary or wall.
cher - ished and freed!
all hu - man - kind.
raise our clear voice!

Community, Freedom

42a From Wisdom Emerging

Galatians 3:28; 1 John 4:16

1. From Wisdom emerging, we fashion a space
for people converging in safety and grace,
to shelter the freedom of one and of all
in Love without border or boundary or wall.

2. Faith's journey reclaiming, we blaze a new trail
with others, exclaiming: "Let justice prevail!"
Rejecting worn paths that oppress and mislead,
we walk in community, cherished and freed!

3. Forever exploring, we seek to learn more
of Wisdom's outpouring, of Love's open door.
Amazed at the mysteries and graces we find,
we joyfully share them with all humankind.

4. The future progressing, we move through its change,
old systems redressing, new patterns arrange;
protecting all freedoms with every new choice,
we follow the Spirit and raise our clear voice!

Words: Larry E. Schultz
Music: Welsh hymn tune

ST. DENIO
11.11.11.11

Our Mother Rock Who Gave Us Birth 43

Deuteronomy 32:18

Descant
4. On Moth - er Rock we can de - pend; She
is our sol - id ground. Her hope for all will
nev - er end; Her love and grace a - bound.
Unison
1. Our Moth - er Rock who gave us birth sup - plies our needs each day. Her nur - ture bless - es all on earth; She is our strength and stay.
2. Our Moth - er Rock on whom we stand sup - ports our jus - tice call. The strong foun - da - tion of each land, She takes down ev - ery wall.
3. Though we for - get Her lov - ing care, Her bless - ings nev - er cease. She gives Her life for all to share, Her ev - er - last - ing peace.
4. On Moth - er Rock we can de - pend; She is our sol - id ground. Her hope for all will nev - er end; Her love and grace a - bound.

Words: Jann Aldredge-Clanton
Music: Larry E. Schultz

BLACK POINT CHURCH
8.6.8.6 (CM)

43a Our Mother Rock Who Gave Us Birth

Deuteronomy 32:18

1. Our Moth-er Rock who gave us birth sup-plies our needs each day.
2. Our Moth-er Rock on whom we stand sup-ports our jus - tice call.
3. Though we for - get Her lov - ing care, Her bless-ings nev - er cease.
4. On Moth-er Rock we can de-pend; She is our sol - id ground.
Her nur - ture bless - es all on earth; She is our strength and stay.
The strong foun - da - tion of each land, She takes down ev - ery wall.
She gives Her life for all to share, Her ev - er - last - ing peace.
Her hope for all will nev - er end; Her love and grace a - bound.

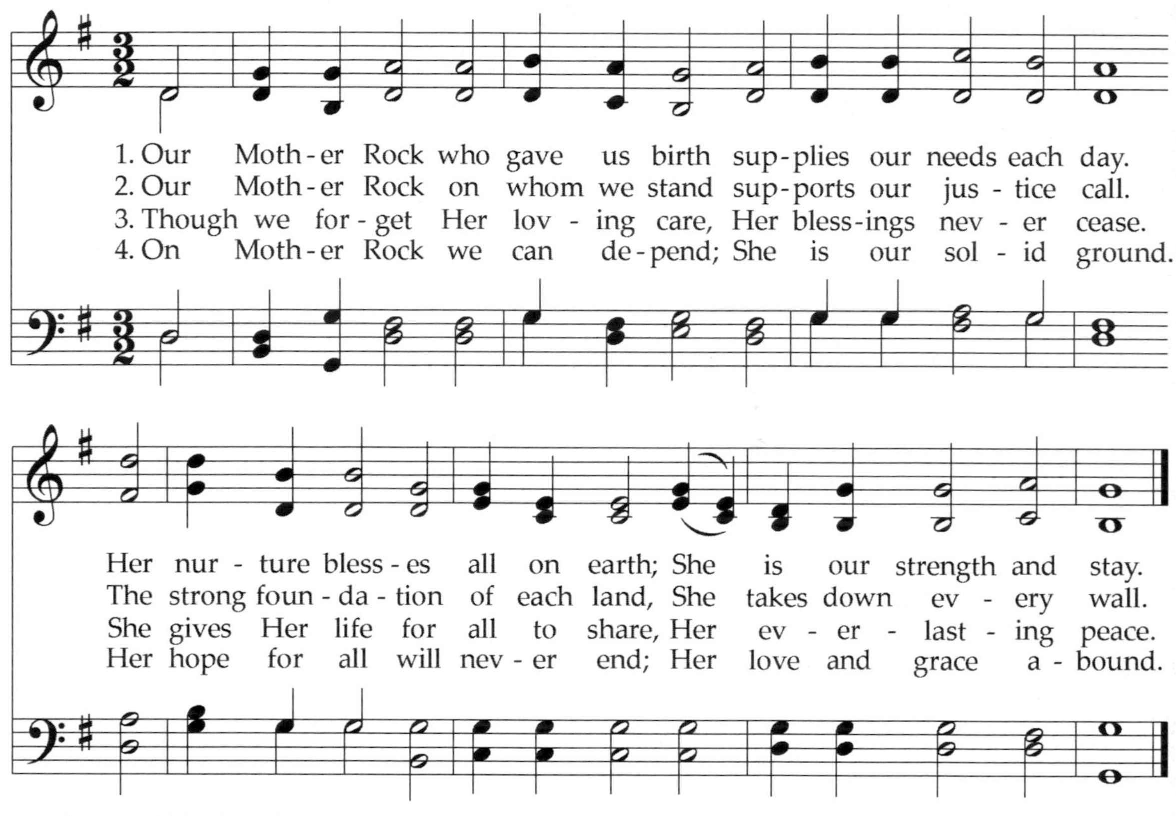

Words: Jann Aldredge-Clanton
Music: Carl G. Gläser; arr. Lowell Mason

AZMON
8.6.8.6 (CM)

Comfort, Hope

Sophia Moves Within Our Souls 44

Sirach 6:25-28, 51:26; Matthew 11:28-29, 23:37; Ephesians 4:15

1. So - phi-a moves with - in our souls to bring us con - so - la - tion;
2. So - phi-a moves through proph - ets bold, who cel - e - brate Her sto-ry;
3. So - phi-a moves through - out the world to bring new rev - e - la - tion;
Her touch of com - fort gives us hope in times of des - o - la - tion.
still some re - fuse Her peace - ful ways, Her gen - tle grace and glo-ry.
we feel Her strong and ten - der touch, re - stor - ing all cre - a - tion.
When we are wea - ry and dis - tressed, our bur-dens She is shar-ing;
To all who join Her jus - tice work, She free - ly gives Her pow - er;
Her heal - ing mis - sion we will join, our deep-est vi - sions bring-ing;
through all the strug - gle and the pain, we feel Her arms of car-ing.
we then can speak the truth in love; our gifts will ful - ly flow - er.
the earth trans-formed with beau - ty blooms, and we re - joice with sing - ing.

Words: Jann Aldredge-Clanton
Music: Robert Lowry

ENDLESS SONG
8.7.8.7 D

Comfort, Hope

45 Gently Shaddai* Comes Healing Wounded Hearts

Genesis 49:25; Isaiah 49:15, 66:13

1. Gen - tly Shad - dai comes heal - ing wound - ed hearts;
2. Glad - ly Shad - dai comes giv - ing lov - ing care,
3. Free - ly Shad - dai pours bless - ings on the earth;
a - bun - dant hope and com - fort She im - parts.
with ten - der pow - er ev - ery bur - den shares.
through night and day She brings new life to birth.
She holds us close through ev - ery pain and grief,
She ful - ly nur - tures ev - ery wea - ry soul;
She fills the world with beau - ty ev - ery - where,
calm - ing our fears and bring - ing deep re - lief.
as we drink deep - ly, we are strong and whole.
with o - ver - flow - ing gifts for all to share.

Words: Jann Aldredge-Clanton
Music: William Henry Monk

Shaddai is a Hebrew name translated "God of the Breasts," "the Breasted God," or "God Almighty."

EVENTIDE
10.10.10.10

Sister Friend, Brother Friend 46

Proverbs 3:17; John 15:12-15

1. Sis - ter Friend, we call on You each day for
2. Broth - er Friend, help us to calm each fear on
3. Broth - er - Sis - ter Friend, we claim Your love to
wis - dom ev - ery hour; Sis - ter Friend, show us Your
paths so hard and long; Broth-er Friend, come now to
take down ev - ery wall; Your life with - in us
peace - ful way and bring Your heal - ing power.
hold us near and keep our cour - age strong.
and a - bove for - ev - er guides us all.

Words: Jann Aldredge-Clanton
Music: Folk melody, Henry Ward Beecher's *Plymouth Collection*, 1855

MAITLAND
8.6.8.6 (CM)

47 Love Divine Is Like a Searching Woman

Luke 15:8-10

1. Love Di - vine is like a Wom - an
2. Still the peas - ant Wom - an search - es,
3. Search - ing Wom - an, Love most Ho - ly,
search - ing long all day and night,
hold - ing up Her lamp of light,
moves through all the world each day,
look - ing for a coin of sil - ver,
look - ing in the far - thest plac - es,
look - ing for the tired and lone - ly,
sweep - ing house with all Her might.
till Her treas - ure comes to sight.
seek - ing all who lost our way.

Words: Jann Aldredge-Clanton
Music: Rowland H. Prichard

HYFRYDOL
8.7.8.7 D

Search - ing, sweep - ing ev - ery cor - ner,
Like the coin, we all are pre - cious;
When She finds us, She re - joic - es;
lis - tening for the faint - est sound,
ev - ery - one has deep - est worth;
heaven and earth will hear Her call,
She will la - bor with - out ceas - ing,
so the Wom - an keeps on search - ing,
"Wel - come ev - ery - one with glad - ness;
till the miss - ing one is found.
cry - ing out through all the earth.
o - pen wide the ban - quet hall."

48 Wisdom Sophia Brings Us Peace

Psalm 85:10-11; Proverbs 3:17; Isaiah 45:3

1. Wis - dom So - phi - a brings us peace,
2. Wis - dom So - phi - a comes to stay,
3. Jus - tice and peace will join in love,
4. Wis - dom So - phi - a fills the earth,
heal - ing our wound - ed hearts.
guid - ing all day and night.
mak - ing Her mes - sage clear.
mak - ing the wound - ed whole.
Her lov - ing care will nev - er cease,
Her Ho - ly Dark - ness shows the Way,
She lives with - in, a - round, a - bove,
Join - ing with Her we bring new birth,
com - fort - ing hope im - parts.
lead - ing to truth and right.
work - ing both far and near.
as we re - store our souls.

Words: Jann Aldredge-Clanton
Music: John Bacchus Dykes

ST. AGNES
8.6.8.6 (CM)

Celebrate Our Maker's Glory 49

Psalm 104:1-25; Isaiah 55:12; Luke 4:18-19; 2 Corinthians 5:17

1. Cel - e - brate our Mak-er's glo - ry, shin - ing bright - ly ev - ery - where;
2. Love Di - vine is like a foun-tain, gush - ing forth un - end - ing streams,
3. Feel the Ho - ly Spir - it's pow - er, deep with - in us and a - bove,
all the world is charged with gran-deur, call - ing for our lov - ing care.
fill - ing earth with lav - ish bless-ings, stir - ring ev - ery - one to dream.
help-ing us dis - cern our mis - sion, guid - ing ev - ery - one to love.
Star - ry skies and gold - en mead-ows, soar - ing ea - gles, leap - ing deer,
Glad - ly shar - ing gifts with oth - ers, we ful - fill our sa - cred call,
Join - ing hands for peace and jus - tice, we will work so all are free,
clap - ping trees and sing - ing moun-tains lift our hearts with hope and cheer.
swing-ing wide the doors of free - dom, bring-ing Good News un - to all.
part - ners in the new cre - a - tion, mak - ing dreams re - al - i - ty.

Words: Jann Aldredge-Clanton
Music: Ludwig van Beethoven

HYMN TO JOY
8.7.8.7 D

50 We Come in Celebration

Proverbs 3:17; Luke 4:18-19; 1 Corinthians 1:24; Galatians 5:1

1. We come in cel - e - bra - tion of bless - ings through the years,
2. As part - ners we will la - bor for free - dom ev - ery - where,
3. Our mis - sion still in - spires us to bring Good News to all,
4. For past and pre-sent vi - sions, for fu - ture dreams held high,
as we have joined to - geth - er on mis - sion far and near.
each voice, each con - gre - ga - tion af - firmed with lov - ing care.
to side with poor and hun - gry to sound the jus - tice call.
we thank You, Ho - ly Wis - dom; on You we still re - ly.
We praise You, Ho - ly Wis - dom, for guid-ance day by day,
We join to work for jus - tice, for heal - ing of the earth;
We work to end op - pres - sion so all are whole and free;
Our grat - i - tude we bring You for cour - age to be free
for var - ied gifts u - nit - ed to make a peace - ful way.
come, Ho - ly Wis - dom, guide us in new cre - a - tion's birth.
come, Ho - ly Wis - dom, help us cre - ate e - qual - i - ty.
to co - cre - ate and nur - ture a bold com - mu - ni - ty.

Words: Jann Aldredge-Clanton
Music: Melchior Teschner

ST. THEODULPH
7.6.7.6 D

With Hearts Overflowing Our Voices We Raise 51

Psalm 100; Luke 4:18-19

1. With hearts o - ver - flow - ing our voic - es we raise;
2. To - geth - er on mis - sion deep mean - ing we find,
3. We come here to cel - e - brate life full and free,
4. This bold con - gre - ga - tion brings jus - tice on earth;
in songs of thanks - giv - ing our Mak - er we praise.
in feed - ing of bod - y and spir - it and mind.
the church ev - er grow - ing to all we can be.
we join Ho - ly Mys - tery in giv - ing new birth.
We gath - er re - joic - ing for grace al - ways near,
Di - verse and cre - a - tive, we fol - low our call,
We join with the Spir - it to dream and to dare,
With love flow - ing free - ly and wel - come for all,
for bless - ings and vi - sions re - ceived through the years.
and join Love Di - vine bring - ing Good News to all.
to bring lov - ing - kind - ness and peace ev - ery - where.
to - geth - er we an - swer the life - giv - ing call.

Words: Jann Aldredge-Clanton
Music: Jeremiah Ingalls' *Christian Harmony*, 1805

I LOVE THEE
11.11.11.11

Call, Vision

52 She Lives!

Proverbs 1:20-25, 3:13-18; Amos 5:24; Micah 6:8

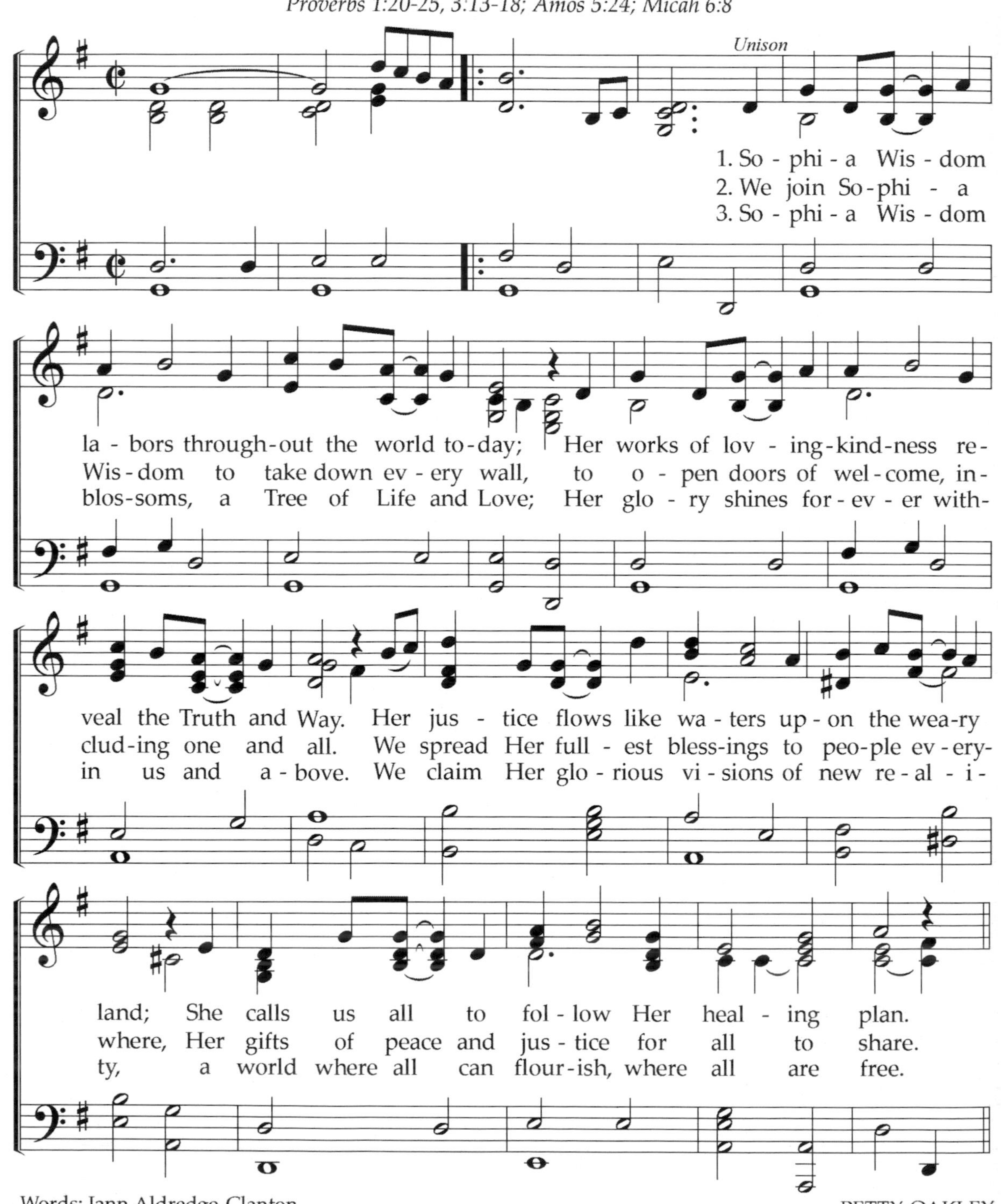
Unison
1. So - phi - a Wis - dom
2. We join So - phi - a
3. So - phi - a Wis - dom
la - bors through-out the world to-day; Her works of lov - ing-kind-ness re-
Wis - dom to take down ev - ery wall, to o - pen doors of wel - come, in-
blos-soms, a Tree of Life and Love; Her glo - ry shines for - ev - er with-
veal the Truth and Way. Her jus - tice flows like wa - ters up - on the wea-ry
clud-ing one and all. We spread Her full - est bless-ings to peo-ple ev - ery-
in us and a - bove. We claim Her glo - rious vi - sions of new re - al - i-
land; She calls us all to fol - low Her heal - ing plan.
where, Her gifts of peace and jus - tice for all to share.
ty, a world where all can flour - ish, where all are free.

Words: Jann Aldredge-Clanton
Music: Larry E. Schultz

PETTY-OAKLEY
Irregular

Descant
She lives, She lives! So - phi - a lives to - day; She lives and works through-
She lives, She lives! So - phi - a lives to - day; She lives and works throughout the world to show the peace - ful way. She lives, She lives! We
out the world to show the peace - ful way. She lives, She lives! We
hear Her ur - gent call; we work with Her to change the world; She lives with -
hear Her ur - gent call; we work with Her to change the world; She lives with -
1, 2.
3.
in us all. in us all.
in us all. in us all.

52a

She Lives!

Proverbs 1:20-25, 3:13-18; Amos 5:24; Micah 6:8

1. Sophia Wisdom labors throughout the world today;
Her works of loving-kindness reveal the Truth and Way.
Her justice flows like waters upon the weary land;
She calls us all to follow Her healing plan. *(Refrain)*

2. We join Sophia Wisdom to take down every wall,
to open doors of welcome, including one and all.
We spread Her fullest blessings to people everywhere,
Her gifts of peace and justice for all to share. *(Refrain)*

3. Sophia Wisdom blossoms, a Tree of Life and Love;
Her glory shines forever within us and above.
We claim Her glorious visions of new reality,
a world where all can flourish, where all are free. *(Refrain)*

Refrain: She lives, She lives! Sophia lives today;
She lives and works throughout the world
to show the peaceful way.
She lives, She lives! We hear Her urgent call;
we work with Her to change the world;
She lives within us all.

Words: Jann Aldredge-Clanton
Music: A. H. Ackley

ACKLEY
7.6.7.6.7.6.7.4 with refrain

Come, Celebrate All Saints 53

Hebrews 12:1-2

Unison
1. Come, cel - e - brate all saints who led the quest, by ac - tions proved the jus - tice they pro - fessed. Their work, O Christ - So - phi - a, You have blessed.
2. You held and nur - tured them through day and night; O Christ - So - phi - a, You gave them new light. Led by Your vi - sion, they preached truth and right.
3. These saints en - gaged the world through mys - tic eyes; they loved all be - ings, heard the poor - est cries. Like them, O Christ - So - phi - a, make us wise.
4. All through the ag - es saints have la - bored long, with deep com - pas - sion kept their voic - es strong, preach - ing for jus - tice, sing - ing peace - ful songs.
5. O may we join these proph - ets from the past, with gen - tle strength, hold our con - vic - tions fast, that free - dom's song we all may sing at last.
Al - le - lu - ia! Al - le - lu - ia!

Words: Jann Aldredge-Clanton
Music: Ralph Vaughan Williams

SINE NOMINE
10.10.10 with alleluias

54 Come and Worship Our Loving Creator

Soprano Descant
Come and wor - ship our Lov-ing Cre-a-tor and Source of all.
Unison Line/Keyboard Part
Come and wor-ship our Lov-ing Cre-a-tor, Moth-er and Fa-ther, Source of our lives.
Bass Line
Come and wor - ship. Come and wor - ship.
Come, dis - cov - er the Spir-it with-in us, our dreams to re-vive.
Come, dis-cov-er the Spir-it with-in us, stir-ring fresh hope, our dreams to re-vive.
Come, dis - cov - er fresh hope, our dreams to re-vive.

Words: Jann Aldredge-Clanton
Music: Larry E. Schultz

Performance Options:
First Time: Unison Line
Second Time: Soprano and Bass Lines
Third Time: All Lines together
(Keyboard plays each time)
or
Unison Line used with litany (opposite pag

Use the unison line from #54 for the sung responses in the following litany:

All: *(singing)*
Come and worship our Loving Creator,
Mother and Father, Source of our lives.
Come, discover the Spirit within us,
stirring fresh hope, our dreams to revive.

Reader 1: To worship is to dance with the Spirit of Love, who is alive in each of us.

All: *(singing)*
Come and worship our Loving Creator,
Mother and Father, Source of our lives.
Come, discover the Spirit within us,
stirring fresh hope, our dreams to revive.

Reader 2: Through worship we speak and sing our visions of the new creation into reality.

All: *(singing)*
Come and worship our Loving Creator,
Mother and Father, Source of our lives.
Come, discover the Spirit within us,
stirring fresh hope, our dreams to revive.

Reader 3: Through worship we breathe the air of a time yet to be, a time when barriers are broken down and wounds are healed.

All: *(singing)*
Come and worship our Loving Creator,
Mother and Father, Source of our lives.
Come, discover the Spirit within us,
stirring fresh hope, our dreams to revive.

Reader 4: Let us celebrate with hope that silenced voices will be heard, trembling voices will be made strong, oppressed people will be set free, so that the Spirit at work yesterday, today, and forever will be proclaimed.

All: *(singing)*
Come and worship our Loving Creator,
Mother and Father, Source of our lives.
Come, discover the Spirit within us,
stirring fresh hope, our dreams to revive.

55 We Come Rejoicing Here Today

Obbligato
Tune
1. We come re - joic - ing here to - day, our
2. How love - ly is Your dwell - ing place, O
3. We find our peace and hope in You, our
songs of glad - ness bring-ing; Your pres - ence in us
Source of all cre - a - tion; our souls are long - ing
strength for all en - deav - ors; O Spir - it liv - ing
o - ver - flows, a well of wis - dom
for Your life of joy and cel - e -
in us all, we sing Your praise for -
spring - ing, a well of wis - dom spring-ing.
bra - tion, of joy and cel - e - bra - tion.
ev - er; we sing Your praise for - ev - er.

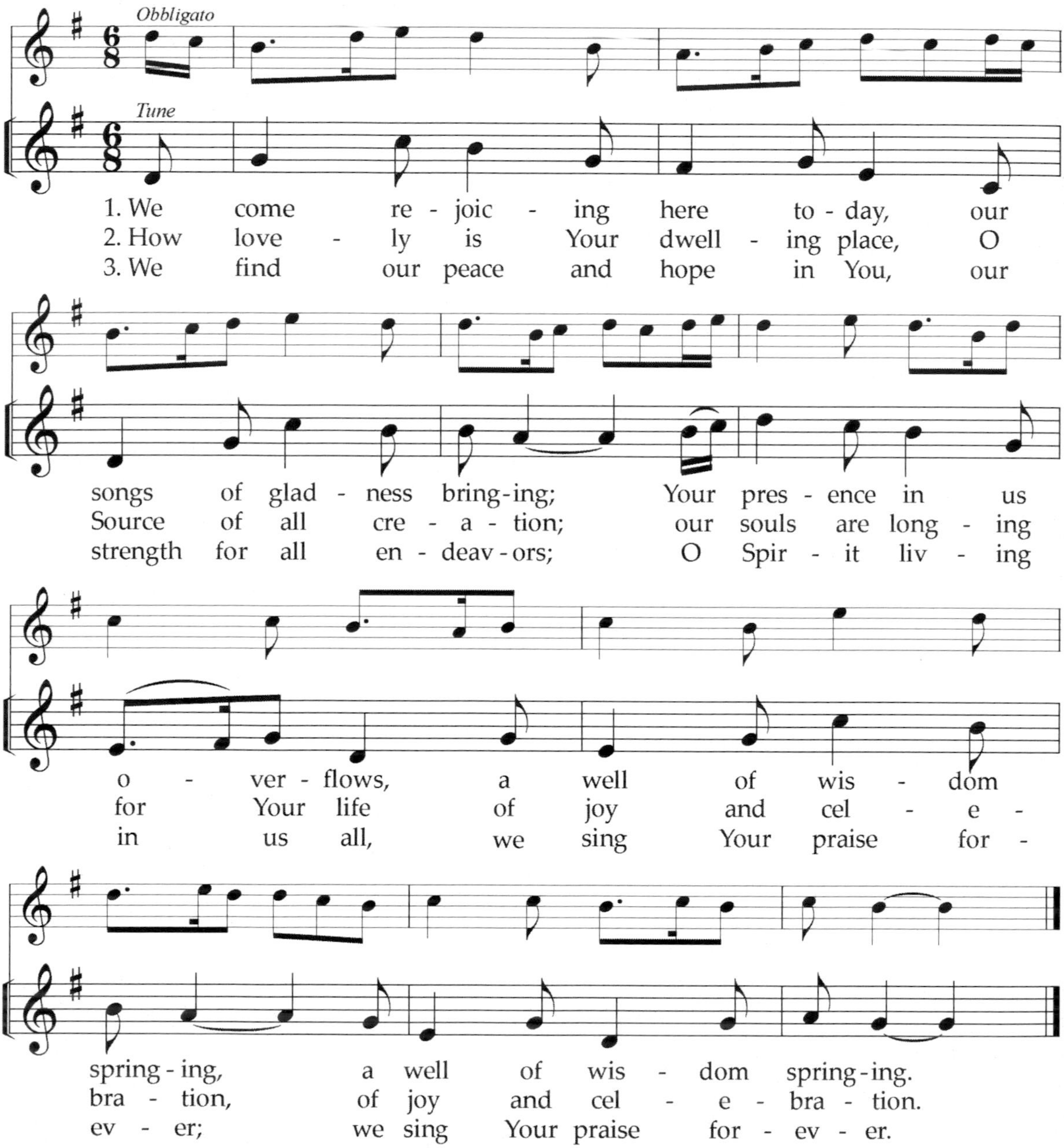

Performance Notes: This folk setting in the style of a jig may incorporate at least two instruments on the tune and obbligato lines to provide introduction and accompaniment. Melodic folk instruments such as fiddle, mandolin, dulcimer fife or pennywhistle are preferred though other C instruments played at any octave may be used. Rhythmic folk instruments such as spoons, drums, shakers, etc. may also be used to provide an underlying dance beat

suggested pattern for rhythm instruments

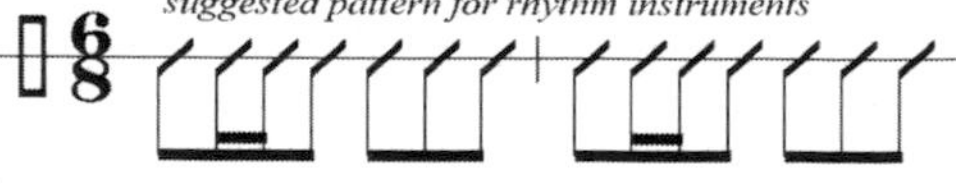

Words: Jann Aldredge-Clanton

Music: Larry E. Schultz

For the Wisdom in the Word 56

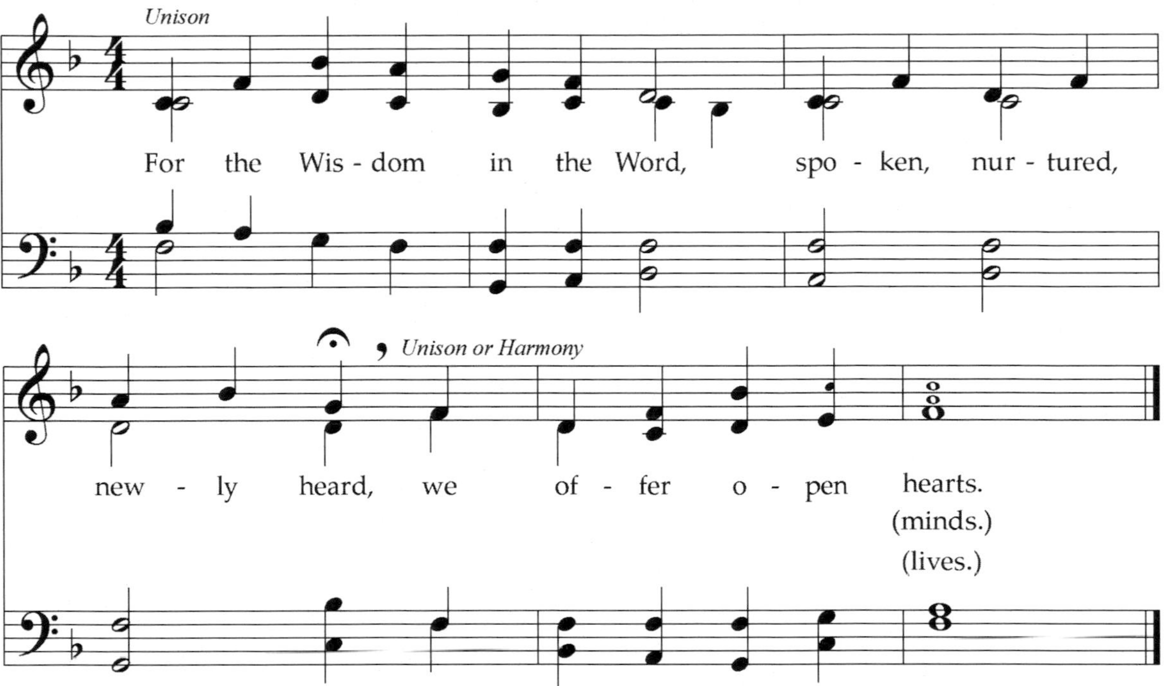
Unison
For the Wis - dom in the Word, spo - ken, nur - tured,
Unison or Harmony
new - ly heard, we of - fer o - pen hearts.
(minds.)
(lives.)

Words and Music: Jann Aldredge-Clanton and Larry E. Schultz

"For the Wisdom in the Word" may be effectively sung as a response to scripture or other worship readings. Alternate endings (hearts, minds, lives) may be selected as appropriate or may be used in response to successive lectionary readings. Additionally, repetition of the song with the different endings may be dispersed throughout a service of worship as follows:

Call to Worship:
For the Wisdom in the Word,
spoken, nurtured, newly heard,
we offer open *hearts.*

Response to Scripture:
For the Wisdom in the Word,
spoken, nurtured, newly heard,
we offer open *minds.*

Sending Out:
For the Wisdom in the Word,
spoken, nurtured, newly heard,
we offer open *lives.*

A soloist (perhaps the reader of scripture) or a choir may offer the opening phrases with the full congregation of worshipers responding with the concluding phrase.
The optional (cue-sized) treble notes at the end "open" the unison line to harmony and may be sung by a choir. This responsive piece may be succesfully sung accompanied or unaccompanied.

57 Rushing Wind, Transforming Fire

1 Unison
2
Rush - ing wind, trans - form - ing fire, with Your power our
souls in - spire; as we come to - geth-er this day,
Spir - it, stir in us, we pray.
Opt. SATB Coda
Spir - it, stir in us, we pray.

Performance Idea: First Time: Unison; Second Time: Two-Part Round as indicated (accompanist repeats measures 7-8 when sung in Round); conclude with SATB Coda (accompanied or unaccompanied)

Words: Jann Aldredge-Clanton

Music: Larry E. Schultz

Sister-Brother Spirit, Within Us and Above 58

Unison
Sis - ter - Broth - er Spir - it, with - in us and a - bove,
show us all Your peace - ful way to part - ner - ship and love;
Sis - ter - Broth - er Spir - it, em - pow - er us to - day;
stir in us new vi - sions of jus - tice, we pray.

Words: Jann Aldredge-Clanton
Music: Larry E. Schultz

Performance Ideas: Sing slowly and expressively as a chant. Tenor/Bass voices singing "oo" or an ethereal organ registration or other instruments may provide a bass clef line accompaniment to unaccompanied treble voices. These voices or instruments may provide an introduction by singing or playing bass clef measures 1-2 two times.

59 Mystery Divine

Opt. Descant on Repeat
Mys-ter - y Di - vine, deep with - in us all as we gath - er here to - day. Shar - ing bread and
to pray. *Mys - ter - y Di -*
Unison
Mys-ter - y Di-vine, deep with - in us all, may we know Your pres - ence as we gath - er here to - day. Shar - ing bread and wine,
to pray. *Mys - ter - y Di - vine,*

Words: Jann Aldredge-Clanton
Music: Larry E. Schultz

Use italic text when sung as a call to prayer.

wine, o-pen to Your call, we seek Your
vine,
o-pen to Your call, we will seek Your wis-dom and Your
wis-dom's peace - ful way.
peace - ful way.

60 As We Come to the Table of Love

Unison
As we come to the ta - ble of Love,
as we come to the ta - ble of Love,
we come with a heart o - pen to
all, as we come to the ta - ble of Love.

Words: Nancy E. Petty
Music: Nancy E. Petty; harm. Larry E. Schultz.

We Come to This Table 61

Unison
We come to this ta - ble with
hope in our hearts, with long-ing for peace that the Spir-it im-parts. We
come with thanks - giv - ing for bread and for wine, for
all of the gifts from the Spir - it Di-vine.

Words: Jann Aldredge-Clanton
Music: Larry E. Schultz

62 Spirit of New Life

Unison
Spir - it of New Life, fill us all, we pray,
as we come to - geth - er at Your ta - ble to - day.

Words: Jann Aldredge-Clanton
Music: Larry E. Schultz

Use #62 for the sung responses in the following litany:

Leader: We give thanks for the invitation to this table, for here we find the Spirit of New Life active in our lives and in this community.

All: *(singing)*
Spirit of New Life, fill us all, we pray,
as we come together at Your table today.

Leader: All are welcome to this table of grace and peace and freedom.

All: *(singing)*
Spirit of New Life, fill us all, we pray,
as we come together at Your table today.

Leader: We share this bread and cup, affirming our connection with Divine Mystery and with one another in this community.

All: *(singing)*
Spirit of New Life, fill us all, we pray,
as we come together at Your table today.

Leader: We come to this table remembering Jesus, who taught us the ways of radical peace and justice and welcome. We eat this bread and drink this cup as Jesus did.

All: *(singing)*
Spirit of New Life, fill us all, we pray,
as we come together at Your table today.

Leader: Our Mother-Father, Sister-Brother, Friend, Guide,
and so much more than we can ever imagine, be with us now.
As we eat this bread and drink this cup, may we remember
that Your Spirit continues to move in our lives in ways beyond our imagining.

All: *(singing)*
Spirit of New Life, fill us all, we pray,
as we come together at Your table today.

63 Come, Sophia Wisdom, Come

Unison
1. Come, So - phi - a Wis-dom, come, live in our hearts;
2. Come, So - phi - a Wis-dom, come, live through-out earth;
come, So-phi - a Wis-dom, come, peace to im - part.
come, So-phi - a Wis-dom, come, bring - ing new birth.
Heal us, bless us, stir us, and free us.
Heal all, bless all, stir all, and free all.
Come, So-phi - a Wis-dom, come, live in our hearts.
Come, So-phi - a Wis-dom, come, live through-out earth.

Words: Jann Aldredge-Clanton
Music: Larry E. Schultz

Go Now with Wisdom

Unison
Go now with Wis-dom on path-ways of peace,
join-ing to-geth-er, all tal-ents re-lease;
spread Wis-dom's mes-sage of fair-ness and love;
fol-low Her call-ing, with-in and a-bove.

Words: Jann Aldredge-Clanton
Music: Traditional Irish melody

65 Go Out with Love

Descant (2nd Time)
Go out with love, free-ly for all; fol - low the Spir - it's call;
Unison
Go out with love flow-ing free-ly for all, fol-low-ing glad-ly the Spir-it's clear call;
go out with joy, vis-ions in-crease; fill the world with jus-tice and peace.
go out with joy as our vi-sions in-crease, fill-ing the world with Her jus-tice and peace.
1.
2.
Go out with love; go with joy; go with peace. peace.
Go out with love; go with joy; go with peace. peace.

Words: Jann Aldredge-Clanton
Music: Larry E. Schultz

NOTES

1. Come, Sing of New Creation

Virginia Baptist Women in Ministry (VBWIM) commissioned this hymn to honor the life and work of one of their founders, Barbara Jackson. She had been active in VBWIM since its inception in 1987. Colleagues described Barbara as a "dedicated servant leader," "bold advocate for the full equality of ministerial leadership of women," "true pioneer," "bridge builder," "humanitarian," and "skilled writer and editor." "Come, Sing of New Creation" was premiered at the VBWIM celebration of Barbara Jackson on May 2, 2014.

2. Renewing, Reforming the Church in Our Day

In 2012, United Theological Seminary sponsored its first annual song and hymn writing competition, "New Songs and Hymns for Renewal," inviting lyricists and composers to submit "songs or hymns with themes of church renewal or personal spiritual renewal." These themes caught my attention because of my writing on changing the church and on deepening spiritual experience through expanding images of the Divine. "Renewing, Reforming the Church in Our Day" won in the category of "New Hymn Text for Traditional Hymn Tune." The judges commented that this text "has outstanding theological significance in church renewal."

3, 3a. Mary Magdalene Inspires Us

Like the Female Divine, many biblical females have been ignored, excluded, demeaned, misinterpreted, and defamed. Mary Magdalene is one of these women. Many theologians and religious leaders, including Pope Gregory in the 6th century, have defamed her as a prostitute. In the 20th century the Vatican finally reversed this judgment of Mary Magdalene, but this misinterpretation of her as a repentant prostitute persists in some religious groups and in the popular media through films like *The Last Temptation of Christ*. This hymn celebrates the prominent part Mary Magdalene plays in the Gospel narratives. "Mary Magdalene Inspires Us" draws from biblical passages that reveal her as among the women disciples who provide for the other disciples and for Jesus, and as the first witness of the resurrection, the "apostle to the apostles."

This hymn can be sung to the tune SPIRIT DANCE by Larry E. Schultz or to his arrangement of the traditional hymn tune BEACH SPRING. Larry originally composed the flowing, vibrant tune SPIRIT DANCE for the hymn "Sister Spirit, Brother Spirit," published in our first hymn collection, *Inclusive Hymns for Liberating Christians* (Eakin Press, 2006).

4. Miriam Shows Us Pathways to Freedom

Miriam is another strong woman whose important part in biblical revelation is often overlooked. This hymn affirms the biblical accounts of Miriam as co-leader of the Exodus, along with Moses and Aaron. Miriam's song, celebrating the exodus victory, is one of the earliest works in Hebrew literature and one of the oldest extant parts of the Bible. In addition to the most often cited story of her protection of baby Moses, this hymn highlights Miriam's role as a prophet and leader.

5. We Gather in a Circle Here

Rev. Stacy Boorn, pastor of Ebenezer/herchurch Lutheran in San Francisco, invited me to take part in a croning ceremony and to write a hymn for this celebration. To challenge patriarchal culture's oppression and demeaning of older women as "useless, unbeautiful has-beens," herchurch has a croning ritual on the 2nd Sunday of Easter each year to celebrate the "wisdom, beauty, and power of elder women." In this ritual a "crone" is defined as one "who is recognized as a wise woman, a spiritual elder, a wise mentor, a treasure of power and wisdom." The ritual affirms "her beauty, her contribution to society, her leadership in the spiritual community, and her ongoing transformation." With this description in mind, I wrote "We Gather in a Circle Here" to celebrate wise women.

6. We Work for Racial Justice Now
7. We Long for Change

These two hymns, like many others in this collection, highlight the intersectionality of racial and gender justice and other forms of justice. Equity for Women in the Church, Inc., which Rev. Sheila Sholes-Ross and I co-chair, inspired these hymns. The big vision of this organization is to facilitate equal representation of clergywomen as pastors of multicultural churches in order to transform church and society. Although many denominations have been ordaining women since the 1950s and 60s and the number of women in theological education has increased to about 40%, only about 10% of pastors of all Protestant churches are women. The percentage of women of color who find places to fulfill their call to pastor is much lower. Equity for Women in the Church works to overcome racism, sexism, and other injustices in order to open doors of opportunity for all who are called and trained to serve as pastors.

11. Praise the Source of All Creation

12. Rejoicing, Reclaiming Our Life-Giving Call

In 2012, the Religious Institute sponsored its first hymn contest on the subject of the gift of sexuality, calling for hymns specifically addressing themes articulated in the Institute's "Declaration on Sexual Morality, Justice, and Healing." Among these themes are working to end sexual abuse and gender violence, and working for full inclusion of women and LGBTQ persons in congregational life, including their ordination and marriage equality. I submitted these two hymn texts to the contest, and "Praise the Source of All Creation" was selected as the winner. When asked by the director of the Religious Institute to comment on the hymn, I wrote: "Words we sing in worship have great power to shape belief and action, helping congregations and individuals in our journey toward healing from sexism, heterosexism, racism, and other injustices. The Religious Institute's prophetic mission inspired my hymn, and I feel honored to contribute to this mission of celebrating the goodness of all creation and affirming a sexual ethic based on justice, equality, and full inclusion of all persons."

15. Where She Dwells, There Is Love

This hymn is dedicated to Marg Herder, who is Director of Public Information for Evangelical & Ecumenical Women's Caucus-Christian Feminism Today (EEWC-CFT) and who is a writer, musician, photographer, sound artist, and activist. Marg inspired this hymn with her blog "Where She Is," through her representation of EEWC-CFT at social justice conferences, and through all her ministries of justice, peace, and love. Marg refers to the Divine Presence with female pronouns, so the title of her blog is "Where She Is." Marg hopes this blog will illuminate Divine Presence and help in what she sees as our ultimate purpose of "allowing our lives to fill with Her love, kindness, and peace."

16. **Where Are Liberty and Justice?**
17. **We Hear the Cries of Millions**
18. **Rise Up and Shout**
19. **Join Together, Work for Justice**
20. **All Who Labor Through Day and Night**

The inspiration for these hymns came from the Dallas Workers' Rights Board. For many years I have served on this Board, which has the goal of bringing together community leaders who are willing to support workers' rights, particularly the rights of workers who do not have the support of strong unions. Members of the Workers' Rights Board include clergy, organizers, activists, educators, lawyers, journalists, and others. The activities of the Workers' Rights Board include hearings where workers present their struggles, speaking out on behalf of workers through writing letters to employers, delegation visits to management or public officials, speaking out through the media, demonstrating solidarity with workers in various other ways, and working closely with North Texas Jobs with Justice on campaigns and issues. "Join Together, Work for Justice" was also inspired by an International Women's Day event titled "Texas Women Inspiring Change," co-sponsored by North Texas Jobs with Justice, and by my participation in events at the UN Commission on the Status of Women. This hymn has been sung at International Women's Day celebrations.

23. **Praise the Source of Every Blessing**
24. **O Earth, We Hear Your Cries of Pain**
25. **Ruah, the Spirit, Dwells**
26. **Sophia Wisdom Shows the Way**

These hymns are inspired by and dedicated to my sister, Dr. Anne Morton, who works tirelessly to save our environment. A local environmental leader, she helped to keep hydraulic fracturing (fracking) out of the city of Dallas.

At the 2012 Faith and Feminism/Womanist/Mujerista Conference, sponsored by Ebenezer/herchurch Lutheran in San Francisco, we sang these hymns in a workshop I led entitled "EcoHymnody." The theme of this conference was "Earth herbody—spirituality, politics and praxis for a sustainable world." The female divine names and images in these hymns connect the revaluing of females and the revaluing of Earth, contributing to overcoming sexism, heterosexism, racism, and exploitation of Earth.

30. Hope Springs Anew

At the 2013 Hymn Society Annual Conference in Richmond, Virginia, I attended a text writers' workshop. Hymn writer Thomas Troeger led the workshop and selected "Hope Springs Anew" as one of the hymns for critique. His helpful suggestions and those of others in the workshop contributed to this hymn.

32. Come, Mother Eagle, Show the Way

This hymn is dedicated to my wonderful grandsons, Lyle, Emmett, and Paul. Mother Eagle is one of their favorite images of the Divine. They delight in singing "Mother Eagle in the Sky," published in *Sing and Dance and Play with Joy! Inclusive Songs for Young Children* (Lulu, 2009). They also love "Mother Eagle, Teach Us to Fly," from *Imagine God! A Children's Musical Exploring and Expressing Images of God* (Choristers Guild, 2004). Larry E. Schultz and I wrote these two works that include female and male images of the Divine to teach children the foundational biblical truth that males and females of all races are created equally in the divine image. Our hope is that through also singing "Come, Mother Eagle, Show the Way" and all the songs in this new collection people of all ages will learn an expansive theology and an ethic of equality and fairness in human relationships.

33. Praise Sophia, Holy Wisdom

This hymn is dedicated to Rev. Stacy Boorn, pastor of Ebenezer/herchurch Lutheran in San Francisco, on the occasion of her 25th anniversary of ministry. These lyrics celebrate Pastor Stacy's 25 years of prophetic ministry in the church and the world. Through her boldness in re-imaging divinity to include female divine names and images, she has brought "inclusive justice" both to the church and the wider culture, supporting "full equality" for all. I am profoundly grateful for Pastor Stacy's prophetic, creative gifts and for her affirmation of my gifts, stirring me to "dream and dare."

36. The Sacred Realm Is Like the Yeast
47. Love Divine Is Like a Searching Woman

These two hymns are inspired by and dedicated to Rev. Gail Ricciuti, who preached a compelling sermon at the Sunday worship service of the 2012 Evangelical & Ecumenical Women's Caucus-Christian Feminism Today Gathering in Indianapolis. Her sermon, entitled "A Quotidian Faith: Stories Sacred, Subversive, and Small," illuminated the female divine images in the parables Jesus told of a woman who stirred yeast in flour, recorded in Luke 13, and of a woman who lost a silver coin, recorded in Luke 15. "The Sacred Realm Is Like the Yeast" and "Love Divine Is Like a Searching Woman" highlight these strong female images of the Divine in the two parables.

38. Our Great Creator Lives in All

This hymn is dedicated to Dr. Kendra Weddle Irons and Dr. Melanie Springer Mock, in celebration of the publication of their book *If Eve Only Knew: Freeing Yourself from Biblical Womanhood and Becoming All God Means for You to Be* (Chalice Press, 2015). This book, like their blog, "Ain't I a Woman," deconstructs messages people get from evangelical popular culture about limited gender roles and constructs a different message that empowers Christian women to be all they are meant to be in the divine image. Kendra asked me to write lyrics to this tune that the popular hymn "And Can it Be" is set to, because she loves this tune but can no longer sing the theology in the hymn. So I wrote "Our Great Creator Lives in All" to this tune. Stanzas one and two especially refer to the prophetic work that Kendra and Melanie do in their teaching, blog, and book, and on the Council of Evangelical & Ecumenical Women's Caucus-Christian Feminism Today (EEWC-CFT).

42, 42a. From Wisdom Emerging

In 2012, the Alliance of Baptists sponsored a hymn contest to celebrate the organization's 25th anniversary. Larry E. Schultz was the winner of this contest with his hymn text "From Wisdom Emerging," set to the tune of ST. DENIO. Permission is granted in perpetuity for this text to be used in gatherings of the Alliance of Baptists and in congregations affiliated with the Alliance of Baptists. This hymn celebrates the Alliance's 25 years of ministry and mission and gives voice to values of the Alliance such as freedom of the individual and the local church, social and economic justice, caring for the earth, honoring wisdom and lifelong learning, and working for peace, equity, and diversity. This hymn was sung at the national Alliance Gathering in 2012 and every year since then. This hymn is also set to the tune VESTA, originally composed by Larry for the hymn "O Loving Creator, We Labor with You," published in our second hymn collection, *Inclusive Hymns for Liberation, Peace, and Justice* (Eakin Press, 2011). This flowing tune also enhances the lyrics of "From Wisdom Emerging." Larry named this tune in memory of his maternal grandmother, Erma Vesta Yarbrough.

43. Our Mother Rock Who Gave Us Birth

Larry E. Schultz originally wrote this tune with a specific text in 2003 as an entry in a hymn contest celebrating the 275th anniversary of First Congregational Church, Scarborough, Maine. BLACK POINT CHURCH, the hymn tune, is a historic name for this church. This tune and text won the church's hymn competition. Larry suggested this tune for my text "Our Strong and Tender God We Praise" in our first hymnbook, *Inclusive Hymns for Liberating Christians*. I selected this tune also for "Our Mother Rock Who Gave Us Birth" because it supports the strong and nurturing images in the text. The descant on the final stanza can make this hymn especially stirring.

49. Celebrate Our Maker's Glory

In 2011, St. Peter's Catholic Church in Charlotte, North Carolina, sponsored a hymn contest in celebration of 25 years of Jesuit leadership, inviting hymns that included "the qualitative aspects of Ignatian spirituality and ministry." This contest attracted my attention because of conversations I'd been having with my son Chad, who was exploring Ignatian spirituality, and because of my love for the poem "God's Grandeur" by Gerard Manley Hopkins, a Jesuit priest, and my appreciation for others of his poems, that I had taught as an English professor at Dallas Baptist University. I especially resonated with the Ignatian beliefs that the Divine lives in all creation and that all people should have freedom to follow their sacred call. I submitted "Celebrate Our Maker's Glory" to the contest and won third place.

50. We Come in Celebration

This hymn won honorable mention in the 2012 Alliance of Baptists hymn contest, which invited hymns to celebrate the Alliance's 25 years of ministry and mission and to give voice to values of the Alliance. Because of their prophetic stands for justice and equality for women, LGBTQ persons, and people of all races, I became affiliated with the Alliance of Baptists as an endorsed chaplain and recognized clergyperson. This hymn celebrates the freedom and other blessings I have experienced in the Alliance, especially the opportunity to "create equality" through Equity for Women in the Church, which is both an Alliance community and an incorporated ecumenical, multicultural organization. "We Come in Celebration" was sung at the national Alliance meeting in 2012 and in meetings since then.

52, 52a. She Lives!

As I was completing my book *She Lives! Sophia Wisdom Works in the World* (Skylight Paths, 2014), I wrote this hymn of celebration. In the introduction of the book I commented on the title: "Growing up in the Baptist tradition, I learned from memory the hymn 'He Lives.' I loved singing this hymn to a lilting tune, increasing in volume along with everyone in the congregation as we came to the refrain which repeats over and over the words 'He lives.' It would not be until many years later that I could even imagine singing or saying, 'She lives.' I had learned to worship a God who was named and imaged as male. But while studying in a conservative Baptist seminary, I was surprised to find Her." I did indeed discover numerous biblical female names and images of the Divine and their connection to social justice, peace, and equality. One of my favorite female names for the Divine is "Wisdom," *Hokmah* in the Hebrew Scriptures and *Sophia* in the Greek language of the Christian Scriptures. The hymn "She Lives!" alludes to Wisdom's works included in the book: gender equality, racial equality, marriage equality, economic justice, care of creation, nonviolence, interfaith collaboration, expansion of spiritual experience, and egalitarian faith communities.

Larry E. Schultz composed a festive new tune for this text in celebration of the marriage of Nancy Petty and Karla Oakley on May 3, 2015. Larry named the tune PETTY-OAKLEY to honor Nancy and Karla, who embody Sophia in their union and in their bold and life-giving ministry.

TOPICAL INDEX OF HYMNS

ADVENT

Come, Join with the Children....27
Hope Springs Anew....30
She Lives and Moves Throughout the Earth....34

ADVERSITY

A Stranger, Starving on the Street....21
All Who Labor Through Day and Night....20
Gently Shaddai Comes Healing Wounded Hearts....45
Holy Wisdom Still Is Calling....28
Longing to Be Free at Last....10
O Earth, We Hear Your Cries of Pain....24
Sister Friend, Brother Friend....46
Sophia Moves Within Our Souls....44
We Hear the Cries of Millions....17
Where Are Liberty and Justice?....16
Who Will Help All Those in Need?....22

ALL SAINTS' DAY

Come, Celebrate All Saints....53

ASSURANCE

A Stranger, Starving on the Street 21
All Day and Night Shekhinah Guides Us 14
Come, Celebrate All Saints 53
Follow Her Peaceful Ways 8, 8a
Gently Shaddai Comes Healing Wounded Hearts 45
Holy Wisdom Still Is Calling 28
Holy, Wondrous Mystery, Birthing All Creation 37
Love Divine Is Like a Searching Woman 47
Mary Magdalene Inspires Us 3, 3a
Our Great Creator Lives in All 38
Our Mother Rock Who Gave Us Birth 43, 43a
Shekhinah Dwells Within Our Hearts 31
Sister Wisdom, Come to Guide Us 29
Sophia Moves Within Our Souls 44
The Sacred Realm Is Like the Yeast 36
We Praise the Source of Life 40
Where Are Liberty and Justice? 16
Where She Dwells, There Is Love 15
Wisdom Sophia Brings Us Peace 48

BEAUTY

Celebrate Our Maker's Glory 49
Come, Join with the Children 27
Come, Mother Eagle, Show the Way 32
Gathered Here to Share Our Music 41
Gently Shaddai Comes Healing Wounded Hearts 45
Holy, Wondrous Mystery, Birthing All Creation 37
Hope Springs Anew 30
In Unity We Gather 39
O Earth, We Hear Your Cries of Pain 24
Our Great Creator Lives in All 38
Our Lady Guadalupe 9
Praise Sophia, Holy Wisdom 33
Praise the Source of All Creation 11

Praise the Source of Every Blessing 23
Ruah, the Spirit, Dwells 25
She Lives! 52, 52a
She Lives and Moves Throughout the Earth 34
Sophia Moves Within Our Souls 44
Sophia Wisdom Shows the Way 26
We Come Rejoicing Here Today 55
We Gather in a Circle Here 5
We Work for Racial Justice Now 6

CALL

A Stranger, Starving on the Street 21
All Who Labor Through Day and Night 20
Celebrate Our Maker's Glory 49
Celebrate This Congregation 13
Come and Worship Our Loving Creator 54
Come, Join with the Children 27
Follow Her Peaceful Ways 8, 8a
For the Wisdom in the Word 56
From Wisdom Emerging 42, 42a
Gathered Here to Share Our Music 41
Go Now with Wisdom 64
Go Out with Love 65
Holy Wisdom Still Is Calling 28
Join Together, Work for Justice 19
Love Divine Is Like a Searching Woman 47
Mary Magdalene Inspires Us 3, 3a
Mystery Divine 59
O Earth, We Hear Your Cries of Pain 24
Our Great Creator Lives in All 38
Our Mother Rock Who Gave Us Birth 43, 43a
Praise Sophia, Holy Wisdom 33
Praise the Source of Every Blessing 23
Rejoicing, Reclaiming Our Life-Giving Call 12
Renewing, Reforming the Church in Our Day 2
Rise Up and Shout 18

Ruah, the Spirit, Dwells 25
She Lives! 52, 52a
She Lives and Moves Throughout the Earth 34
Sister Friend, Brother Friend 46
Sister Wisdom, Come to Guide Us 29
Sophia Wisdom Shows the Way 26
We Hear the Cries of Millions 17
Where Are Liberty and Justice? 16
Where She Dwells, There Is Love 15
Who Will Help All Those in Need? 22
With Hearts Overflowing Our Voices We Raise 51

CARE OF CREATION (see also Earth Day)

Celebrate Our Maker's Glory 49
Come, Join with the Children 27
Follow Her Peaceful Ways 8, 8a
O Earth, We Hear Your Cries of Pain 24
Praise Sophia, Holy Wisdom 33
Praise the Source of Every Blessing 23
Ruah, the Spirit, Dwells 25
Shekhinah Dwells Within Our Hearts 31
Sophia Wisdom Shows the Way 26
We Come in Celebration 50

CARING FOR OTHERS

A Stranger, Starving on the Street 21
All Day and Night Shekhinah Guides Us 14
As We Come to the Table of Love 60
Celebrate Our Maker's Glory 49
Celebrate This Congregation 13
Come, Celebrate All Saints 53
Come, Join with the Children 27
Follow Her Peaceful Ways 8, 8a
From Wisdom Emerging 42, 42a
Go Out with Love 65

Holy Wisdom Still Is Calling 28
Join Together, Work for Justice 19
Praise Sophia, Holy Wisdom 33
Renewing, Reforming the Church in Our Day 2
Rise Up and Shout 18
She Lives! 52, 52a
We Hear the Cries of Millions 17
We Long for Change 7
Where Are Liberty and Justice? 16
Where She Dwells, There Is Love 15
Who Will Help All Those in Need? 22

CELEBRATION (see also Praise)

A Stranger, Starving on the Street 21
Celebrate Our Maker's Glory 49
Celebrate This Congregation 13
Come and Worship Our Loving Creator 54
Come Rejoicing, Celebrating Life Together 35
Come, Sing of New Creation 1
From Wisdom Emerging 42, 42a
Gathered Here to Share Our Music 41
Go Out with Love 65
Holy, Wondrous Mystery, Birthing All Creation 37
Hope Springs Anew 30
In Unity We Gather 39
Love Divine Is Like a Searching Woman 47
Miriam Shows Us Pathways to Freedom 4
Our Great Creator Lives in All 38
Praise Sophia, Holy Wisdom 33
Praise the Source of All Creation 11
Praise the Source of Every Blessing 23
Rejoicing, Reclaiming Our Life-Giving Call 12
She Lives! 52, 52a
She Lives and Moves Throughout the Earth 34
Shekhinah Dwells Within Our Hearts 31
We Come in Celebration 50

We Come Rejoicing Here Today 55
We Gather in a Circle Here 5
We Praise the Source of Life 40
With Hearts Overflowing Our Voices We Raise 51

CHALLENGE

A Stranger, Starving on the Street 21
All Who Labor Through Day and Night 20
Come Rejoicing, Celebrating Life Together 35
Come, Sing of New Creation 1
Follow Her Peaceful Ways 8, 8a
From Wisdom Emerging 42, 42a
Holy Wisdom Still Is Calling 28
Join Together, Work for Justice 19
Miriam Shows Us Pathways to Freedom 4
O Earth, We Hear Your Cries of Pain 24
Our Great Creator Lives in All 38
Our Lady Guadalupe 9
Praise Sophia, Holy Wisdom 33
Praise the Source of Every Blessing 23
Rejoicing, Reclaiming Our Life-Giving Call 12
Renewing, Reforming the Church in Our Day 2
Rise Up and Shout 18
Ruah, the Spirit, Dwells 25
She Lives! 52, 52a
She Lives and Moves Throughout the Earth 34
Sister Friend, Brother Friend 46
Sister Wisdom, Come to Guide Us 29
Sophia Wisdom Shows the Way 26
We Hear the Cries of Millions 17
We Long for Change 7
We Work for Racial Justice Now 6
Where Are Liberty and Justice? 16
Who Will Help All Those in Need? 22

COMFORT

All Day and Night Shekhinah Guides Us 14
Gently Shaddai Comes Healing Wounded Hearts 45
Love Divine Is Like a Searching Woman 47
Sister Friend, Brother Friend 46
Sister Wisdom, Come to Guide Us 29
Sophia Moves Within Our Souls 44
Wisdom Sophia Brings Us Peace 48

COMMUNION

A Stranger, Starving on the Street 21
As We Come to the Table of Love 60
Celebrate This Congregation 13
From Wisdom Emerging 42, 42a
Mystery Divine 59
Spirit of New Life 62
The Sacred Realm Is Like the Yeast 36
We Come to This Table 61
With Hearts Overflowing Our Voices We Raise 51

COMMUNITY

A Stranger, Starving on the Street 21
All Who Labor Through Day and Night 20
As We Come to the Table of Love 60
Celebrate This Congregation 13
Come, Join with the Children 27
Come Rejoicing, Celebrating Life Together 35
Come, Sing of New Creation 1
From Wisdom Emerging 42, 42a
Gathered Here to Share Our Music 41
Go Now with Wisdom 64
In Unity We Gather 39
Join Together, Work for Justice 19

Mary Magdalene Inspires Us 3, 3a
Praise Sophia, Holy Wisdom 33
Renewing, Reforming the Church in Our Day....... 2
She Lives!....... 52, 52a
Spirit of New Life 62
We Come in Celebration 50
We Gather in a Circle Here 5
We Long for Change....... 7
We Work for Racial Justice Now 6
Where She Dwells, There Is Love 15
With Hearts Overflowing Our Voices We Raise....... 51

COURAGE

All Day and Night Shekhinah Guides Us 14
All Who Labor Through Day and Night....... 20
Come, Sing of New Creation 1
From Wisdom Emerging....... 42, 42a
Holy Wisdom Still Is Calling 28
Longing to Be Free at Last....... 10
Miriam Shows Us Pathways to Freedom 4
Our Great Creator Lives in All 38
Our Mother Rock Who Gave Us Birth 43, 43a
Praise the Source of Every Blessing 23
Ruah, the Spirit, Dwells 25
Shekhinah Dwells Within Our Hearts 31
Sister Friend, Brother Friend 46
Sister Wisdom, Come to Guide Us 29
Sophia Wisdom Shows the Way....... 26
We Come in Celebration 50
Where Are Liberty and Justice?....... 16
With Hearts Overflowing Our Voices We Raise....... 51

COVENANT

From Wisdom Emerging....... 42, 42a
O Earth, We Hear Your Cries of Pain....... 24

Praise the Source of Every Blessing 23
Renewing, Reforming the Church in Our Day 2
Ruah, the Spirit, Dwells 25
We Come in Celebration 50
With Hearts Overflowing Our Voices We Raise 51

CREATION

Celebrate Our Maker's Glory 49
Come and Worship Our Loving Creator 54
Come, Join with the Children 27
From Wisdom Emerging 42, 42a
Gathered Here to Share Our Music 41
Holy, Wondrous Mystery, Birthing All Creation 37
Hope Springs Anew 30
In Unity We Gather 39
O Earth, We Hear Your Cries of Pain 24
Our Great Creator Lives in All 38
Our Lady Guadalupe 9
Praise the Source of All Creation 11
Praise the Source of Every Blessing 23
Ruah, the Spirit, Dwells 25
She Lives! 52, 52a
Sophia Moves Within Our Souls 44
Sophia Wisdom Shows the Way 26
We Come in Celebration 50
We Come Rejoicing Here Today 55

CREATIVITY

A Stranger, Starving on the Street 21
Celebrate This Congregation 13
Come Rejoicing, Celebrating Life Together 35
Come, Sing of New Creation 1
From Wisdom Emerging 42, 42a
Gathered Here to Share Our Music 41
Holy, Wondrous Mystery, Birthing All Creation 37

In Unity We Gather 39
Miriam Shows Us Pathways to Freedom 4
Our Lady Guadalupe... 9
Praise Sophia, Holy Wisdom 33
Praise the Source of All Creation 11
Ruah, the Spirit, Dwells 25
Sophia Wisdom Shows the Way... 26
The Sacred Realm Is Like the Yeast... 36
We Come in Celebration 50
We Gather in a Circle Here 5
With Hearts Overflowing Our Voices We Raise... 51

DIVERSITY (see Unity and Diversity)

DIVINE IMAGES

Baker Woman
The Sacred Realm Is Like the Yeast 36
Bread of Life
Mary Magdalene Inspires Us... 3, 3a
The Sacred Realm Is Like the Yeast 36
Breath
Holy, Wondrous Mystery, Birthing All Creation 37
Brother Friend
Sister Friend, Brother Friend... 46
Brother-Sister Spirit
We Hear the Cries of Millions... 17
We Long for Change 7
Christ
A Stranger, Starving on the Street 21
Christ-Sophia
Come, Celebrate All Saints 53
Mary Magdalene Inspires Us... 3, 3a
Praise Sophia, Holy Wisdom... 33
Creative Love
In Unity We Gather 39

Creative Mystery
In Unity We Gather....39
Creative Spirit
In Unity We Gather....39
Praise the Source of All Creation....11
Praise the Source of Every Blessing....23
Creative Wisdom
In Unity We Gather....39
Creator
Come and Worship Our Loving Creator....54
Our Great Creator Lives in All....38
Darkness
Holy, Wondrous Mystery, Birthing All Creation....37
Divine Mystery
Spirit of New Life....62
Earth
O Earth, We Hear Your Cries of Pain....24
Praise the Source of Every Blessing....23
Sophia Wisdom Shows the Way....26
El Shaddai
She Lives and Moves Throughout the Earth....34
Father
Come and Worship Our Loving Creator....54
Friend
Praise Sophia, Holy Wisdom....33
Spirit of New Life....62
Great Mother
We Praise the Source of Life....40
Guide
Gathered Here to Share Our Music....41
Praise Sophia, Holy Wisdom....33
Spirit of New Life....62
Hokmah
She Lives and Moves Throughout the Earth....34
Holy Darkness
Wisdom Sophia Brings Us Peace....48

Holy Mystery
Come Rejoicing, Celebrating Life Together....35
With Hearts Overflowing Our Voices We Raise....51
Holy Spirit
Celebrate Our Maker's Glory....49
Holy Way
Praise the Source of Every Blessing....23
Holy Wisdom
Celebrate This Congregation....13
Come Rejoicing, Celebrating Life Together....35
Come, Sing of New Creation....1
Follow Her Peaceful Ways....8, 8a
Holy Wisdom Still Is Calling....28
Hope Springs Anew....30
Join Together, Work for Justice....19
Mary Magdalene Inspires Us....3, 3a
Praise Sophia, Holy Wisdom....33
Praise the Source of All Creation....11
She Lives and Moves Throughout the Earth....34
We Come in Celebration....50
Where Are Liberty and Justice?....16
Who Will Help All Those in Need?....22
Life
Who Will Help All Those in Need?....22
Living Word
Mary Magdalene Inspires Us....3, 3a
Love
As We Come to the Table of Love....60
From Wisdom Emerging....42, 42a
Renewing, Reforming the Church in Our Day....2
Where She Dwells, There Is Love....15
Love Divine
Celebrate Our Maker's Glory....49
Love Divine Is Like a Searching Woman....47
With Hearts Overflowing Our Voices We Raise....51
Maker
Celebrate Our Maker's Glory....49
Celebrate This Congregation....13

Rejoicing, Reclaiming Our Life-Giving Call....12
With Hearts Overflowing Our Voices We Raise....51

Mary Queen
Our Great Creator Lives in All....38
She Lives and Moves Throughout the Earth....34

Midwife
Praise Sophia, Holy Wisdom....33

Mother
Come and Worship Our Loving Creator....54
Praise Sophia, Holy Wisdom....33
We Praise the Source of Life....40

Mother Eagle
Come, Mother Eagle, Show the Way....32

Mother-Father
Spirit of New Life....62

Mother Hen
She Lives and Moves Throughout the Earth....34

Mother Rock
Our Mother Rock Who Gave Us Birth.... 43, 43a

Mystery
Holy, Wondrous Mystery, Birthing All Creation....37

Mystery Divine
Mystery Divine....59

Our Lady Guadalupe
Our Lady Guadalupe....9

Presence
Holy, Wondrous Mystery, Birthing All Creation....37

Queen
She Lives and Moves Throughout the Earth....34

Revelation
Holy, Wondrous Mystery, Birthing All Creation....37

Risen One
Mary Magdalene Inspires Us....3, 3a

Ruah
Come, Join with the Children....27
Longing to Be Free at Last....10
Our Great Creator Lives in All....38

Ruah, the Spirit, Dwells 25
She Lives and Moves Throughout the Earth 34

Searching Woman

Love Divine Is Like a Searching Woman 47

Shaddai

Gently Shaddai Comes Healing Wounded Hearts 45

She Who Is

Praise Sophia, Holy Wisdom 33

Shekhinah

All Day and Night Shekhinah Guides Us 14
Our Great Creator Lives in All 38
Praise Sophia, Holy Wisdom 33
Shekhinah Dwells Within Our Hearts 31

Sister-Brother

Spirit of New Life 62

Sister-Brother Spirit

Celebrate This Congregation 13
Come Rejoicing, Celebrating Life Together 35
Sister-Brother Spirit, Within Us and Above 58
We Hear the Cries of Millions 17
We Work for Racial Justice Now 6

Sister Friend

She Lives and Moves Throughout the Earth 34
Sister Friend, Brother Friend 46

Sister Wisdom

Sister Wisdom, Come to Guide Us 29

Song of All Life

Holy, Wondrous Mystery, Birthing All Creation 37

Sophia

Come, Sophia Wisdom, Come 63
Praise Sophia, Holy Wisdom 33
She Lives! 52, 52a
She Lives and Moves Throughout the Earth 34
Sophia Moves Within Our Souls 44
Sophia Wisdom Shows the Way 26
We Gather in a Circle Here 5
Wisdom Sophia Brings Us Peace 48

Source
Come and Worship Our Loving Creator ... 54
Praise the Source of All Creation ... 11
Praise the Source of Every Blessing ... 23
We Come Rejoicing Here Today ... 55
Source of All Life
Holy, Wondrous Mystery, Birthing All Creation ... 37
Source of Life
We Praise the Source of Life ... 40
Spirit
All Who Labor Through Day and Night ... 20
Come and Worship Our Loving Creator ... 54
Come, Join with the Children ... 27
From Wisdom Emerging ... 42, 42a
Gathered Here to Share Our Music ... 41
Go Out with Love ... 65
Holy, Wondrous Mystery, Birthing All Creation ... 37
Longing to Be Free at Last ... 10
Miriam Shows Us Pathways to Freedom ... 4
Rejoicing, Reclaiming Our Life-Giving Call ... 12
Renewing, Reforming the Church in Our Day ... 2
Rushing Wind, Transforming Fire ... 57
She Lives and Moves Throughout the Earth ... 34
Spirit of New Life ... 62
We Come Rejoicing Here Today ... 55
We Come to This Table ... 61
Where She Dwells, There Is Love ... 15
With Hearts Overflowing Our Voices We Raise ... 51
Spirit Divine
We Come to This Table ... 61
Spirit of Love
Come and Worship Our Loving Creator ... 54
Spirit of New Life
Spirit of New Life ... 62
Tree of Life
Follow Her Peaceful Ways ... 8, 8a
She Lives! ... 52, 52a
She Lives and Moves Throughout the Earth ... 34

Truth
She Lives! ... 52, 52a
Who Will Help All Those in Need? ... 22
Way
Mary Magdalene Inspires Us ... 3, 3a
Praise Sophia, Holy Wisdom ... 33
Renewing, Reforming the Church in Our Day ... 2
She Lives! ... 52, 52a
Who Will Help All Those in Need? ... 22
Wisdom Sophia Brings Us Peace ... 48
Well of Holy Wisdom
Praise the Source of Every Blessing ... 23
Wisdom
Come, Sing of New Creation ... 1
Come, Sophia Wisdom, Come ... 63
Follow Her Peaceful Ways ... 8, 8a
For the Wisdom in the Word ... 56
From Wisdom Emerging ... 42, 42a
Go Now with Wisdom ... 64
Holy Wisdom Still Is Calling ... 28
Hope Springs Anew ... 30
Mary Magdalene Inspires Us ... 3, 3a
Rise Up and Shout ... 18
She Lives! ... 52, 52a
Sophia Wisdom Shows the Way ... 26
We Gather in a Circle Here ... 5
Who Will Help All Those in Need? ... 22
Wisdom Sophia Brings Us Peace ... 48
Wisdom-Word
She Lives and Moves Throughout the Earth ... 34
Word
For the Wisdom in the Word ... 56
Mary Magdalene Inspires Us ... 3, 3a

DOUBT

Gently Shaddai Comes Healing Wounded Hearts 45
Rise Up and Shout 18
Sister Friend, Brother Friend 46
Sophia Moves Within Our Souls 44

EARTH DAY (see also Care of Creation)

Celebrate Our Maker's Glory 49
Come, Join with the Children 27
Follow Her Peaceful Ways 8, 8a
O Earth, We Hear Your Cries of Pain 24
Praise the Source of Every Blessing 23
Ruah, the Spirit, Dwells 25
Shekhinah Dwells Within Our Hearts 31
Sophia Wisdom Shows the Way 26
We Come in Celebration 50

EASTER (see also Resurrection)

Hope Springs Anew 30
Mary Magdalene Inspires Us 3, 3a
She Lives! 52, 52a
The Sacred Realm Is Like the Yeast 36

EPIPHANY

A Stranger, Starving on the Street 21
Come, Mother Eagle, Show the Way 32
Come, Sing of New Creation 1
From Wisdom Emerging 42, 42a
Holy, Wondrous Mystery, Birthing All Creation 37
Our Great Creator Lives in All 38
Our Lady Guadalupe 9
She Lives! 52, 52a
The Sacred Realm Is Like the Yeast 36

ETERNAL LIFE

Follow Her Peaceful Ways 8, 8a
Holy, Wondrous Mystery, Birthing All Creation 37
Our Mother Rock Who Gave Us Birth 43, 43a
Renewing, Reforming the Church in Our Day 2
She Lives! 52, 52a

FAITH AND TRUST

All Day and Night Shekhinah Guides Us 14
From Wisdom Emerging 42, 42a
Gathered Here to Share Our Music 41
In Unity We Gather 39
Mary Magdalene Inspires Us 3, 3a
Our Mother Rock Who Gave Us Birth 43, 43a
Sister Friend, Brother Friend 46
Where Are Liberty and Justice? 16
We Come in Celebration 50

FORGIVENESS

All Day and Night Shekhinah Guides Us 14
Gathered Here to Share Our Music 41
Our Mother Rock Who Gave Us Birth 43, 43a
Praise the Source of All Creation 11
Rejoicing, Reclaiming Our Life-Giving Call 12
Renewing, Reforming the Church in Our Day 2
Sister Friend, Brother Friend 46
We Long for Change 7

FREEDOM (see also Liberation)

A Stranger, Starving on the Street 21
All Day and Night Shekhinah Guides Us 14
Celebrate Our Maker's Glory 49
Celebrate This Congregation 13

Come and Worship Our Loving Creator 54
Come, Celebrate All Saints 53
Come Rejoicing, Celebrating Life Together 35
Come, Sing of New Creation 1
Come, Sophia Wisdom, Come 63
From Wisdom Emerging 42, 42a
Gathered Here to Share Our Music 41
In Unity We Gather 39
Join Together, Work for Justice 19
Longing to Be Free at Last 10
Miriam Shows Us Pathways to Freedom 4
Our Great Creator Lives in All 38
Praise Sophia, Holy Wisdom 33
Praise the Source of All Creation 11
Renewing, Reforming the Church in Our Day 2
She Lives! 52, 52a
She Lives and Moves Throughout the Earth 34
Sister Wisdom, Come to Guide Us 29
Spirit of New Life 62
We Come in Celebration 50
We Gather in a Circle Here 5
We Long for Change 7
We Work for Racial Justice Now 6
Who Will Help All Those in Need? 22
With Hearts Overflowing Our Voices We Raise 51

GIVING AND RECEIVING (see also Stewardship)

A Stranger, Starving on the Street 21
All Day and Night Shekhinah Guides Us 14
Follow Her Peaceful Ways 8, 8a
Gathered Here to Share Our Music 41
Go Out with Love 65
In Unity We Gather 39
Mary Magdalene Inspires Us 3, 3a
Praise Sophia, Holy Wisdom 33
Renewing, Reforming the Church in Our Day 2

She Lives! 52, 52a
The Sacred Realm Is Like the Yeast 36
We Hear the Cries of Millions 17
Where Are Liberty and Justice? 16
Where She Dwells, There Is Love 15
Who Will Help All Those in Need? 22
With Hearts Overflowing Our Voices We Raise 51

GRACE

A Stranger, Starving on the Street 21
All Day and Night Shekhinah Guides Us 14
Celebrate This Congregation 13
Follow Her Peaceful Ways 8, 8a
From Wisdom Emerging 42, 42a
Gathered Here to Share Our Music 41
Hope Springs Anew 30
O Earth, We Hear Your Cries of Pain 24
Our Mother Rock Who Gave Us Birth 43, 43a
Praise Sophia, Holy Wisdom 33
Praise the Source of All Creation 11
Renewing, Reforming the Church in Our Day 2
Shekhinah Dwells Within Our Hearts 31
Sister Friend, Brother Friend 46
Sister Wisdom, Come to Guide Us 29
Sophia Moves Within Our Souls 44
Spirit of New Life 62
We Long for Change 7
With Hearts Overflowing Our Voices We Raise 51

GRIEF

All Day and Night Shekhinah Guides Us 14
Gently Shaddai Comes Healing Wounded Hearts 45
O Earth, We Hear Your Cries of Pain 24
Sophia Moves Within Our Souls 44
Wisdom Sophia Brings Us Peace 48

GUIDANCE AND CARE

A Stranger, Starving on the Street 21
All Day and Night Shekhinah Guides Us 14
Celebrate This Congregation 13
Come, Mother Eagle, Show the Way 32
Come Rejoicing, Celebrating Life Together 35
Come, Sing of New Creation 1
Follow Her Peaceful Ways 8, 8a
From Wisdom Emerging 42, 42a
Gently Shaddai Comes Healing Wounded Hearts 45
Hope Springs Anew 30
Join Together, Work for Justice 19
Longing to Be Free at Last 10
Miriam Shows Us Pathways to Freedom 4
Our Great Creator Lives in All 38
Praise the Source of Every Blessing 23
She Lives and Moves Throughout the Earth 34
Shekhinah Dwells Within Our Hearts 31
Sister Friend, Brother Friend 46
Sister Wisdom, Come to Guide Us 29
Sophia Wisdom Shows the Way 26
We Come in Celebration 50
We Gather in a Circle Here 5
We Hear the Cries of Millions 17
We Work for Racial Justice Now 6
Where She Dwells, There Is Love 15
Wisdom Sophia Brings Us Peace 48

HEALING

A Stranger, Starving on the Street 21
All Day and Night Shekhinah Guides Us 14
Celebrate This Congregation 13
Come and Worship Our Loving Creator 54
Come, Sophia Wisdom, Come 63
From Wisdom Emerging 42, 42a

Gathered Here to Share Our Music 41
Gently Shaddai Comes Healing Wounded Hearts 45
Holy Wisdom Still Is Calling 28
Hope Springs Anew 30
O Earth, We Hear Your Cries of Pain 24
Our Lady Guadalupe 9
Praise the Source of All Creation 11
Praise the Source of Every Blessing 23
Rejoicing, Reclaiming Our Life-Giving Call 12
Renewing, Reforming the Church in Our Day 2
Ruah, the Spirit, Dwells 25
She Lives! 52, 52a
Sister Friend, Brother Friend 46
Sister Wisdom, Come to Guide Us 29
Sophia Moves Within Our Souls 44
We Come in Celebration 50
We Praise the Source of Life 40
We Work for Racial Justice Now 6
Where She Dwells, There Is Love 15
Wisdom Sophia Brings Us Peace 48

HOPE

All Day and Night Shekhinah Guides Us 14
All Who Labor Through Day and Night 20
Come and Worship Our Loving Creator 54
Come Rejoicing, Celebrating Life Together 35
Come, Sing of New Creation 1
Gathered Here to Share Our Music 41
Gently Shaddai Comes Healing Wounded Hearts 45
Holy, Wondrous Mystery, Birthing All Creation 37
Hope Springs Anew 30
In Unity We Gather 39
Longing to Be Free at Last 10
Love Divine Is Like a Searching Woman 47
Mary Magdalene Inspires Us 3, 3a
Miriam Shows Us Pathways to Freedom 4

O Earth, We Hear Your Cries of Pain 24
Our Great Creator Lives in All 38
Our Mother Rock Who Gave Us Birth 43, 43a
Praise Sophia, Holy Wisdom 33
Praise the Source of All Creation 11
Rejoicing, Reclaiming Our Life-Giving Call 12
She Lives and Moves Throughout the Earth 34
Shekhinah Dwells Within Our Hearts 31
Sister Friend, Brother Friend 46
Sister Wisdom, Come to Guide Us 29
Sophia Moves Within Our Souls 44
Sophia Wisdom Shows the Way 26
We Come Rejoicing Here Today 55
We Come to This Table 61
We Praise the Source of Life 40
Who Will Help All Those in Need? 22
Wisdom Sophia Brings Us Peace 48

INCARNATION

A Stranger, Starving on the Street 21
All Day and Night Shekhinah Guides Us 14
Come Rejoicing, Celebrating Life Together 35
Come, Sophia Wisdom, Come 63
Holy, Wondrous Mystery, Birthing All Creation 37
Love Divine Is Like a Searching Woman 47
Mystery Divine 59
Our Great Creator Lives in All 38
Praise the Source of All Creation 11
She Lives and Moves Throughout the Earth 34
Shekhinah Dwells Within Our Hearts 31
Sister Friend, Brother Friend 46
Sister Wisdom, Come to Guide Us 29
The Sacred Realm Is Like the Yeast 36
We Gather in a Circle Here 5
Where She Dwells, There Is Love 15
Wisdom Sophia Brings Us Peace 48

INVITATION

A Stranger, Starving on the Street 21
All Who Labor Through Day and Night 20
Come, Join with the Children 27
Come, Sing of New Creation 1
Follow Her Peaceful Ways 8, 8a
Holy Wisdom Still Is Calling 28
Our Great Creator Lives in All 38
Praise the Source of Every Blessing 23
Rise Up and Shout 18
Ruah, the Spirit, Dwells 25
She Lives! 52, 52a
She Lives and Moves Throughout the Earth 34
Sophia Wisdom Shows the Way 26
We Hear the Cries of Millions 17
Who Will Help All Those in Need? 22

JOY

A Stranger, Starving on the Street 21
Come, Join with the Children 27
Come, Mother Eagle, Show the Way 32
From Wisdom Emerging 42, 42a
Gathered Here to Share Our Music 41
Go Out with Love 65
In Unity We Gather 39
Hope Springs Anew 30
Love Divine Is Like a Searching Woman 47
Mary Magdalene Inspires Us 3, 3a
Miriam Shows Us Pathways to Freedom 4
Our Great Creator Lives in All 38
Praise the Source of All Creation 11
We Come in Celebration 50
We Come Rejoicing Here Today 55

LABOR

All Who Labor Through Day and Night....20
Come, Celebrate All Saints....53
Come, Join with the Children....27
Come, Sing of New Creation....1
Follow Her Peaceful Ways....8, 8a
Gathered Here to Share Our Music....41
Holy, Wondrous Mystery, Birthing All Creation....37
Join Together, Work for Justice....19
Love Divine Is Like a Searching Woman....47
Our Great Creator Lives in All....38
Our Lady Guadalupe....9
Praise the Source of Every Blessing....23
Rejoicing, Reclaiming Our Life-Giving Call....12
Renewing, Reforming the Church in Our Day....2
Rise Up and Shout....18
She Lives!....52, 52a
We Come in Celebration....50
We Hear the Cries of Millions....17
We Long for Change....7
We Praise the Source of Life....40
We Work for Racial Justice Now....6
Where Are Liberty and Justice?....16
Who Will Help All Those in Need?....22

LAMENT

Holy Wisdom Still Is Calling....28
O Earth, We Hear Your Cries of Pain....24
We Hear the Cries of Millions....17
Where Are Liberty and Justice?....16

LENT

A Stranger, Starving on the Street....21
Holy Wisdom Still Is Calling....28

LIBERATION

LOVE

Follow Her Peaceful Ways 8, 8a
From Wisdom Emerging 42, 42a
Holy Wisdom Still Is Calling 28
Holy, Wondrous Mystery, Birthing All Creation 37
Gathered Here to Share Our Music 41
Gently Shaddai Comes Healing Wounded Hearts 45
Go Now with Wisdom 64
Go Out with Love 65
Hope Springs Anew 30
In Unity We Gather 39
Love Divine Is Like a Searching Woman 47
Our Great Creator Lives in All 38
Our Lady Guadalupe 9
Our Mother Rock Who Gave Us Birth 43, 43a
Praise Sophia, Holy Wisdom 33
Praise the Source of All Creation 11
Praise the Source of Every Blessing 23
Rejoicing, Reclaiming Our Life-Giving Call 12
Renewing, Reforming the Church in Our Day 2
Rise Up and Shout 18
She Lives! 52, 52a
She Lives and Moves Throughout the Earth 34
Shekhinah Dwells Within Our Hearts 31
Sister-Brother Spirit, Within Us and Above 58
Sister Friend, Brother Friend 46
Sister Wisdom, Come to Guide Us 29
Sophia Moves Within Our Souls 44
The Sacred Realm Is Like the Yeast 36
We Come in Celebration 50
We Gather in a Circle Here 5
We Hear the Cries of Millions 17
We Long for Change 7
We Praise the Source of Life 40
Where Are Liberty and Justice? 16
Where She Dwells, There Is Love 15
Who Will Help All Those in Need? 22
Wisdom Sophia Brings Us Peace 48
With Hearts Overflowing Our Voices We Raise 51

MINISTRY

A Stranger, Starving on the Street 21
Come, Sing of New Creation 1
Follow Her Peaceful Ways 8, 8a
From Wisdom Emerging 42, 42a
Our Great Creator Lives in All 38
Praise Sophia, Holy Wisdom 33
We Hear the Cries of Millions 17
Who Will Help All Those in Need? 22

MIRACLE

A Stranger, Starving on the Street 21
From Wisdom Emerging 42, 42a
Holy, Wondrous Mystery, Birthing All Creation 37
Hope Springs Anew 30
Mary Magdalene Inspires Us 3, 3a
Our Great Creator Lives in All 38
Our Lady Guadalupe 9
The Sacred Realm Is Like the Yeast 36

MISSION

All Who Labor Through Day and Night 20
Celebrate Our Maker's Glory 49
Celebrate This Congregation 13
Come Rejoicing, Celebrating Life Together 35
Come, Sing of New Creation 1
Holy Wisdom Still Is Calling 28
Join Together, Work for Justice 19
Mary Magdalene Inspires Us 3, 3a
Our Great Creator Lives in All 38
Our Lady Guadalupe 9
Praise Sophia, Holy Wisdom 33
Praise the Source of All Creation 11
Renewing, Reforming the Church in Our Day 2

Rise Up and Shout 18
Ruah, the Spirit, Dwells 25
She Lives! 52, 52a
Shekhinah Dwells Within Our Hearts 31
Sophia Moves Within Our Souls 44
Sophia Wisdom Shows the Way 26
We Come in Celebration 50
We Praise the Source of Life 40
With Hearts Overflowing Our Voices We Raise 51

NEW CREATION

Celebrate Our Maker's Glory 49
Come and Worship Our Loving Creator 54
Come, Mother Eagle, Show the Way 32
Come Rejoicing, Celebrating Life Together 35
Come, Sing of New Creation 1
Gathered Here to Share Our Music 41
Holy Wisdom Still Is Calling 28
Praise Sophia, Holy Wisdom 33
Renewing, Reforming the Church in Our Day 2
She Lives! 52, 52a
She Lives and Moves Throughout the Earth 34
Sister Wisdom, Come to Guide Us 29
We Come in Celebration 50
Wisdom Sophia Brings Us Peace 48

NEW LIFE

All Day and Night Shekhinah Guides Us 14
Celebrate This Congregation 13
Come, Join with the Children 27
Come, Sophia Wisdom, Come 63
Follow Her Peaceful Ways 8, 8a
For the Wisdom in the Word 56
From Wisdom Emerging 42, 42a
Gently Shaddai Comes Healing Wounded Hearts 45

Holy Wisdom Still Is Calling 28
Holy, Wondrous Mystery, Birthing All Creation 37
Hope Springs Anew 30
Join Together, Work for Justice 19
Longing to Be Free at Last 10
Mary Magdalene Inspires Us 3, 3a
O Earth, We Hear Your Cries of Pain 24
Our Great Creator Lives in All 38
Praise Sophia, Holy Wisdom 33
Praise the Source of All Creation 11
Praise the Source of Every Blessing 23
Rejoicing, Reclaiming Our Life-Giving Call 12
Ruah, the Spirit, Dwells 25
She Lives! 52, 52a
She Lives and Moves Throughout the Earth 34
Sophia Wisdom Shows the Way 26
Spirit of New Life 62
We Gather in a Circle Here 5
We Praise the Source of Life 40
Who Will Help All Those in Need? 22
Wisdom Sophia Brings Us Peace 48
With Hearts Overflowing Our Voices We Raise 51

ONENESS

In Unity We Gather 39
Our Great Creator Lives in All 38
Rejoicing, Reclaiming Our Life-Giving Call 12
Renewing, Reforming the Church in Our Day 2
We Praise the Source of Life 40

PARTNERSHIP

All Who Labor Through Day and Night 20
Celebrate Our Maker's Glory 49
Celebrate This Congregation 13
Come, Join with the Children 27

Come, Mother Eagle, Show the Way 32
Follow Her Peaceful Ways 8, 8a
From Wisdom Emerging 42, 42a
In Unity We Gather 39
Join Together, Work for Justice 19
Miriam Shows Us Pathways to Freedom 4
Our Great Creator Lives in All 38
Praise the Source of All Creation 11
Praise the Source of Every Blessing 23
Rejoicing, Reclaiming Our Life-Giving Call 12
Renewing, Reforming the Church in Our Day 2
Rise Up and Shout 18
She Lives! 52, 52a
Sister-Brother Spirit, Within Us and Above 58
Sister Wisdom, Come to Guide Us 29
We Come in Celebration 50
We Gather in a Circle Here 5
We Hear the Cries of Millions 17
We Praise the Source of Life 40
We Work for Racial Justice Now 6
Where Are Liberty and Justice? 16

PEACE

All Day and Night Shekhinah Guides Us 14
Celebrate Our Maker's Glory 49
Celebrate This Congregation 13
Come, Mother Eagle, Show the Way 32
Come Rejoicing, Celebrating Life Together 35
Come, Sophia Wisdom, Come 63
Follow Her Peaceful Ways 8, 8a
Gathered Here to Share Our Music 41
Go Now with Wisdom 64
Go Out with Love 65
Holy Wisdom Still Is Calling 28
Hope Springs Anew 30
In Unity We Gather 39

PENTECOST

POWER

All Day and Night Shekhinah Guides Us 14
All Who Labor Through Day and Night 20
Celebrate Our Maker's Glory 49
Celebrate This Congregation 13
Come Rejoicing, Celebrating Life Together 35
Come, Sing of New Creation 1
Follow Her Peaceful Ways 8, 8a
Gathered Here to Share Our Music 41
Gently Shaddai Comes Healing Wounded Hearts 45
Miriam Shows Us Pathways to Freedom 4
O Earth, We Hear Your Cries of Pain 24
Our Great Creator Lives in All 38
Our Lady Guadalupe 9
Praise Sophia, Holy Wisdom 33
Ruah, the Spirit, Dwells 25
Rushing Wind, Transforming Fire 57
She Lives! 52, 52a
Shekhinah Dwells Within Our Hearts 31
Sister-Brother Spirit, Within Us and Above 58
Sister Friend, Brother Friend 46
Sister Wisdom, Come to Guide Us 29
Sophia Moves Within Our Souls 44
We Come in Celebration 50
We Gather in a Circle Here 5
We Hear the Cries of Millions 17
We Long for Change 7
We Praise the Source of Life 40
We Work for Racial Justice Now 6
Where Are Liberty and Justice? 16

PRAISE (see also Thanksgiving)

Holy, Wondrous Mystery, Birthing All Creation 37
In Unity We Gather 39
Praise Sophia, Holy Wisdom 33

Praise the Source of All Creation 11
Praise the Source of Every Blessing 23
She Lives! 52, 52a
We Come in Celebration 50
We Come Rejoicing Here Today 55
We Praise the Source of Life 40
With Hearts Overflowing Our Voices We Raise 51

PRAYER

Come, Mother Eagle, Show the Way 32
Come, Sophia Wisdom, Come 63
Longing to Be Free at Last 10
Mystery Divine 59
Our Lady Guadalupe 9
Rushing Wind, Transforming Fire 57
Sister-Brother Spirit, Within Us and Above 58
Sister Friend, Brother Friend 46
Sister Wisdom, Come to Guide Us 29
Spirit of New Life 62
We Come in Celebration 50
We Hear the Cries of Millions 17
We Long for Change 7
Where Are Liberty and Justice? 16

RENEWAL

A Stranger, Starving on the Street 21
All Day and Night Shekhinah Guides Us 14
Come and Worship Our Loving Creator 54
Come Rejoicing, Celebrating Life Together 35
Come, Sing of New Creation 1
From Wisdom Emerging 42, 42a
Gently Shaddai Comes Healing Wounded Hearts 45
Hope Springs Anew 30
Love Divine Is Like a Searching Woman 47
Our Great Creator Lives in All 38

Our Lady Guadalupe...9
Praise Sophia, Holy Wisdom 33
Praise the Source of All Creation 11
Rejoicing, Reclaiming Our Life-Giving Call...12
Renewing, Reforming the Church in Our Day..2
Ruah, the Spirit, Dwells 25
Rushing Wind, Transforming Fire..57
She Lives!.. 52, 52a
She Lives and Moves Throughout the Earth 34
Sister Wisdom, Come to Guide Us 29
Sophia Moves Within Our Souls...44
Sophia Wisdom Shows the Way..26
The Sacred Realm Is Like the Yeast..36
We Gather in a Circle Here 5
We Long for Change...7
Where She Dwells, There Is Love 15
Wisdom Sophia Brings Us Peace 48

REPENTANCE (see Forgiveness)

RESURRECTION (see also Easter)

Hope Springs Anew...30
Mary Magdalene Inspires Us 3, 3a
The Sacred Realm Is Like the Yeast..36

SOCIAL JUSTICE

All Who Labor Through Day and Night..20
Celebrate Our Maker's Glory...49
Celebrate This Congregation 13
Come, Celebrate All Saints..53
Come, Mother Eagle, Show the Way 32
Come, Sing of New Creation 1
Follow Her Peaceful Ways...8, 8a
From Wisdom Emerging.. 42, 42a
Go Now with Wisdom 64

STEWARDSHIP (see also Giving and Receiving; Creation)

THANKSGIVING

A Stranger, Starving on the Street 21
Celebrate Our Maker's Glory 49
Come, Celebrate All Saints 53
From Wisdom Emerging 42, 42a
Holy, Wondrous Mystery, Birthing All Creation 37
Miriam Shows Us Pathways to Freedom 4
O Earth, We Hear Your Cries of Pain 24
Praise Sophia, Holy Wisdom 33
Praise the Source of Every Blessing 23
We Come in Celebration 50
We Come to This Table 61
With Hearts Overflowing Our Voices We Raise 51

TRINITY

Celebrate Our Maker's Glory 49
Celebrate This Congregation 13
Come Rejoicing, Celebrating Life Together 35
With Hearts Overflowing Our Voices We Raise 51

TRUTH

All Who Labor Through Day and Night 20
Come, Celebrate All Saints 53
Our Great Creator Lives in All 38
She Lives! 52, 52a
Sophia Moves Within Our Souls 44
Where Are Liberty and Justice? 16
Who Will Help All Those in Need? 22
Wisdom Sophia Brings Us Peace 48

UNITY AND DIVERSITY

All Who Labor Through Day and Night 20
As We Come to the Table of Love 60

Celebrate This Congregation 13
From Wisdom Emerging 42, 42a
Gathered Here to Share Our Music 41
In Unity We Gather 39
Our Great Creator Lives in All 38
Praise the Source of All Creation 11
Renewing, Reforming the Church in Our Day 2
Rise Up and Shout 18
We Come in Celebration 50
We Hear the Cries of Millions 17
We Praise the Source of Life 40
Where Are Liberty and Justice? 16
With Hearts Overflowing Our Voices We Raise 51

VISION

A Stranger, Starving on the Street 21
Celebrate This Congregation 13
Come and Worship Our Loving Creator 54
Come, Celebrate All Saints 53
Come, Mother Eagle, Show the Way 32
Come Rejoicing, Celebrating Life Together 35
Come, Sing of New Creation 1
From Wisdom Emerging 42, 42a
Go Out with Love 65
In Unity We Gather 39
Join Together, Work for Justice 19
Longing to Be Free at Last 10
Mary Magdalene Inspires Us 3, 3a
Our Great Creator Lives in All 38
Our Lady Guadalupe 9
Praise Sophia, Holy Wisdom 33
Renewing, Reforming the Church in Our Day 2
She Lives! 52, 52a
She Lives and Moves Throughout the Earth 34
Sister-Brother Spirit, Within Us and Above 58
Sophia Moves Within Our Souls 44
We Come in Celebration 50

We Gather in a Circle Here 5
We Work for Racial Justice Now 6
With Hearts Overflowing Our Voices We Raise 51

WHOLENESS

All Day and Night Shekhinah Guides Us 14
Gently Shaddai Comes Healing Wounded Hearts 45
Praise the Source of All Creation 11
Rejoicing, Reclaiming Our Life-Giving Call 12
Sophia Moves Within Our Souls 44

INDEX OF SCRIPTURE REFERENCES

Genesis

1 .... 27, 37
1:1-2 40
1:1-27 11
1:27 .... 6, 12
1:29-31 24
1:31 .... 11, 12
49:25 45

Exodus

2:1-10 4
6:2-8 6
15:20-21 4
16:1-12 10
29:45 .... 14, 31
40:34-38 .... 14, 31, 33

Deuteronomy

32:11-12 32
32:18 .... 43, 43a
34:1-4 10

Psalms

22:9-10 33
85:10-11 48
92:12-14 5
100 51
104:1-25 49
104:5-30 24
104:10-25 23
133:1 .... 39, 40
139:12 9

Proverbs

1:20-23 .... 3, 3a, 8, 8a, 16, 18, 28, 34
1:20-25 .... 52, 52a
3:13-18 .... 8, 8a, 11, 16, 18, 19, 29, 52, 52a
3:17 .... 3, 3a, 38, 39, 46, 48, 50
3:17-18 .... 1, 22, 23, 26, 28, 30, 33, 34, 35
4:10-18 22
7:4 29
8:23 5

Sirach

6:25-28 44
51:26 44

Isaiah

35:1-7 25
35:1-10 .... 23, 30
45:3 .... 37, 48
49:15 45
55:12 .... 39, 49
55:12-13 .... 30, 38
58:6-8 30
65:17-25 28
66:13 .... 33, 45

Amos

4:1 16
5:11-12 .... 16, 17
5:21-24 17
5:24 .... 16, 52, 52a

Micah

6:4 4
6:8 .... 52, 52a

Matthew

5:9 .... 3, 3a
11:28-29 44
23:37 44
25:35-40 21

Luke

1:26-55 9
4:18 .... 7, 13, 18, 22
4:18-19 .... 2, 49, 50, 51
8:1-3 .... 3, 3a
13:20-21 36
15:8-10 47
24:13-35 21

John

10:34 38
15:15 33
15:12-15 46
20:1-18 .... 3, 3a

Acts

2:17 .... 1, 5
2:17-18 7

1 Corinthians

1:24 .... 3, 3a, 50
12:4-31 13
13:13 39

2 Corinthians

5:17 .... 1, 2, 32, 35, 41, 49

Galatians

3:28 .... 42, 42a
5:1 50
5:22 .... 20, 41
5:25 20

Ephesians

4:15 44

Hebrews

12:1-2 53

1 John

4:16 .... 15, 42, 42a
4:16-21 40

Revelation

21:1-6 13

INDEX OF COMPOSERS, AUTHORS, AND SOURCES

African-American spiritual....20
Bach, Johann Sebastian (1685-1750)....17
Beethoven, Ludwig van (1770-1827)....33, 49
Bliss, Philip P. (1838-1876)....15
Campbell, Thomas (1777-1844)....38
Chorale melodien zum heiligen Gesange (1808)....34
Christian Harmony (Jeremiah Ingalls, 1805)....51
Dare, Elkanah Kelsay (1782-1826)....31
Durham, Matilda T. (1815-1901)....6
Dutch melody....41
Dykes, John Bacchus (1823-1876)....37, 48
English Country Songs (English Traditional, 1893)....21
Folk melody....46
Gauntlett, Henry J. (1805-1876)....29
Genuine Church Music (Joseph Funk, 1832)....12
Gläser, Carl G. (1784-1829)....43a
Goss, John (1800-1880)....23
Hassler, Hans Leo (1564-1612)....17
Haydn, Franz Joseph (1732-1809)....19
Irish melody....32
Lowry, Robert (1826-1899)....24, 44
Malan, César (1787-1864)....22
Mason, Lowell (1792-1872)....43a
Monk, William Henry (1823-1889)....45
Mozart, Wolfgang Amadeus (1756-1791)....28

Neumark, Georg (1621-1681) 14
Petty, Nancy E. (1963-) 60
Plymouth Collection (Henry Ward Beecher, 1855) 46
Prichard, Rowland H. (1811-1887) 11, 47
Psalmodia Evangelica (Thomas Williams, 1789) 30
Repository of Sacred Music, Part Second (Wyeth, 1813) 31, 35
Schultz, Larry E. (1965-) 3, 3a, 8, 21, 37, 42, 42a, 43, 52, 54, 55, 56, 57, 58, 59, 60, 61, 62, 63, 65
Schulz, Johann A.P. (1747-1800) 27
Showalter, A. J. (1858-1924) 10
Smart, Henry T. (1813-1879) 39
Southern Harmony (1835) 6
Tallis, Thomas (ca. 1505-1585) 5
Teschner, Melchior (1584-1635) 50
Thesaurus Musicus (1744) 25
Towner, Daniel B. (1850-1919) 18
Traditional Gaelic melody 4
Traditional Irish melody 7, 36, 64
Vaughan Williams, Ralph (1872-1958) 53
Ward, Samuel A. (1847-1903) 26
Welsh hymn tune 2, 42a
Wesley, Samuel S. (1810-1876) 9
White, B.F. (1800-1879) 3a
Williams, Aaron (1731-1776) 40
Williams, Thomas John (1869-1944) 16
Wittenberg Gesangbuch (1784) 1
Zundel, John (1815-1882) 13

ALPHABETICAL INDEX OF TUNES

AMERICA, 6.6.4.6.6.6.4 25
AURELIA, 7.6.7.6 D 9
AUSTRIAN HYMN, 8.7.8.7 D 19
AZMON, 8.6.8.6 (CM) 43a
BEACH SPRING, 8.7.8.7 D 3a
BEECHER, 8.7.8.7 D 13
BLACK POINT CHURCH, 8.6.8.6 (CM) 43
BUNESSAN, 5.5.5.4 D 4
CLONMEL, 8.6.8.6 D (CMD) 36
EBENEZER, 8.7.8.7 D 16
ELLACOMBE, 7.6.7.6 D 1
ELLESDIE, 8.7.8.7 D 28
ENDLESS SONG, 8.7.8.7 D 24, 44
EVENTIDE, 10.10.10.10 45
FOUNDATION, 11.11.11.11 12
HENDON, 7.7.7.7.7 22
HYFRYDOL, 8.7.8.7 D 11, 47
HYMN TO JOY, 8.7.8.7 D 33, 49
I LOVE THEE, 11.11.11.11 51
IN BABILONE, 8.7.8.7 D 41
IRBY, 8.7.8.7.7.7 29
KINGSFOLD, 8.6.8.6 D (CMD) 21
LANCASHIRE, 7.6.7.6 D 39
LAUDA ANIMA, 8.7.8.7.8.7 23

LONDONDERRY AIR, 11.10.11.10 with refrain 7
MAITLAND, 8.6.8.6 (CM) 46
MATERNA, 8.6.8.6 D (CMD) 26
MORNING SONG, 8.6.8.6.8.6 31
NETTLETON, 8.7.8.7 D 35
NEUMARK, 9.8.9.8.8.8 14
NICAEA, Irregular 37
PASSION CHORALE, 7.6.7.6 D 17
PEACEFUL WAYS, 11.10.11.10 with refrain 8
PETTY-OAKLEY, Irregular 52
PROMISED LAND, 8.6.8.6 (CM) with refrain 6
SAGINA, 8.8.8.8.8.8 with refrain 38
SALVE REGINA COELITUM, 8.4.8.4.7.7.7.6.6 34
SCHULZ, 6.5.6.5 D 27
SHOWALTER, 10.9.10.9 with refrain 10
SINE NOMINE, 10.10.10 with alleluias 53
SOJOURNER, 8.8.8.9 20
SPIRIT DANCE, 8.7.8.7 D 3
ST. AGNES, 8.6.8.6 (CM) 48
ST. COLUMBA, 8.7.8.7 32
ST. DENIO, 11.11.11.11 .... 2, 42a
ST. THEODULPH, 7.6.7.6 D 50
ST. THOMAS, 6.6.8.6 (SM) 40
TALLIS' CANON, 8.8.8.8 (LM) 5
TRURO, 8.8.8.8 (LM) 30
TRUST AND OBEY, Irregular 18
VESTA, 11.11.11.11 42
VILLE DU HAVRE, 11.8.11.9 with refrain 15

METRICAL INDEX OF TUNES

5.5.5.4 D
BUNESSAN ... 4

6.5.6.5 D
SCHULZ ... 27

6.6.4.6.6.6.4
AMERICA ... 25

6.6.8.6 (SM)
ST. THOMAS ... 40

7.6.7.6 D
AURELIA ... 9
ELLACOMBE ... 1
LANCASHIRE ... 39
PASSION CHORALE ... 17
ST. THEODULPH ... 50

7.7.7.7.7
HENDON ... 22

8.4.8.4.7.7.7.6.6
SALVE REGINA COELITUM ... 34

8.6.8.6 (CM)
AZMON ... 43a
BLACK POINT CHURCH ... 43
MAITLAND ... 46
ST. AGNES ... 48

8.6.8.6 (CM) with refrain
PROMISED LAND ... 6

8.6.8.6 D (CMD)
CLONMEL ... 36
KINGSFOLD ... 21
MATERNA ... 26

8.6.8.6.8.6
MORNING SONG ... 31

8.7.8.7
ST. COLUMBA ... 32

8.7.8.7 D
AUSTRIAN HYMN ... 19
BEACH SPRING ... 3a
BEECHER ... 13
EBENEZER ... 16

ELLESDIE 28
ENDLESS SONG 24, 44
HYFRYDOL 11, 47
HYMN TO JOY 33, 49
IN BABILONE 41
NETTLETON 35
SPIRIT DANCE 3

8.7.8.7.7.7
IRBY 29

8.7.8.7.8.7
LAUDA ANIMA 23

8.8.8.8 (LM)
TALLIS' CANON 5
TRURO 30

8.8.8.8.8.8 with refrain
SAGINA 38

8.8.8.9
SOJOURNER 20

9.8.9.8.8.8
NEUMARK 14

10.9.10.9 with refrain
SHOWALTER 10

10.10.10 with alleluias
SINE NOMINE 53

10.10.10.10
EVENTIDE 45

11.8.11.9 with refrain
VILLE DU HAVRE 15

11.10.11.10 with refrain
LONDONDERRY AIR 7
PEACEFUL WAYS 8

11.11.11.11
FOUNDATION 12
I LOVE THEE 51
ST. DENIO 2, 42a
VESTA 42

Irregular
NICAEA 37
PETTY-OAKLEY 52
TRUST AND OBEY 18

INDEX OF TITLES

A Stranger, Starving on the Street 21
All Day and Night Shekhinah Guides Us 14
All Who Labor Through Day and Night 20
As We Come to the Table of Love 60
Celebrate Our Maker's Glory 49
Celebrate This Congregation 13
Come and Worship Our Loving Creator 54
Come, Celebrate All Saints 53
Come, Join with the Children 27
Come, Mother Eagle, Show the Way 32
Come Rejoicing, Celebrating Life Together 35
Come, Sing of New Creation 1
Come, Sophia Wisdom, Come 63
Follow Her Peaceful Ways 8, 8a
For the Wisdom in the Word 56
From Wisdom Emerging 42, 42a
Gathered Here to Share Our Music 41
Gently Shaddai Comes Healing Wounded Hearts 45
Go Now with Wisdom 64
Go Out with Love 65
Holy Wisdom Still Is Calling 28
Holy, Wondrous Mystery, Birthing All Creation 37
Hope Springs Anew 30
In Unity We Gather 39